Snap Beads

Snap Beads

A Remembering

LYNETTE RIGGS

RESOURCE *Publications* • Eugene, Oregon

SNAP BEADS
A Remembering

Copyright © 2024 Lynette Riggs. All rights reserved. Except for brief quotations in critical publications or reviews, no part of this book may be reproduced in any manner without prior written permission from the publisher. Write: Permissions, Wipf and Stock Publishers, 199 W. 8th Ave., Suite 3, Eugene, OR 97401.

Resource Publications
An Imprint of Wipf and Stock Publishers
199 W. 8th Ave., Suite 3
Eugene, OR 97401

www.wipfandstock.com

PAPERBACK ISBN: 979-8-3852-1584-3
HARDCOVER ISBN: 979-8-3852-1585-0
EBOOK ISBN: 979-8-3852-1586-7

05/22/24

The events are based on the author's memories, and any recall errors are the author's own. Some identifying names and details have been changed or omitted to protect the privacy of individuals.

"In the end, we all become stories."
—Margaret Atwood

Contents

	Preface: Just is: Time, Memory, and Genre	ix
1	Refuse	1
2	Dear Baby Girl	2
3	Anita	4
4	Artifacts	6
5	Daddy	8
6	Places and Things	11
7	Mama's Make-up	14
8	The Mustard Seed	16
9	Mississippi	17
10	Hide and Seek	19
11	Tending Momma	21
12	Grandma Leona	23
13	The Gargoyle Upstairs	25
14	Whiffenpoof	28
15	Lost	30
16	White's Motel	32
17	Too-ra-loo-ra-loo-ral	35
18	Hair	37
19	Suicide	39
20	Things	42
21	Maybe	44
22	A Heavy Stone	46

Contents

23	Covenants	48
24	Families are Forever	50
25	Spin the Bottle	52
26	Segregation	55
27	Residential "School"	57
28	Howey Academy	60
29	Finding Peace	63
30	Heavenly Father, Are You Really There?	65
31	Wellsville	67
32	Paul McCartney Eyes	69
33	Christmas 1970	71
34	Becoming a Wife	72
35	Snap Beads	74
36	Sunrise, Sunset, and So Forth	77
37	New Year's Eve	79
38	The Hour of Lead	82
39	Before And After	84
40	Fire!	86
41	Finding My Mother	88
42	Another Lie	90
43	Another Story	92
44	Graveside Services #1 and #2	94
45	Graveside Service #3	96
46	Trunk #3	97
47	Beginning From This Morning	99
	Bibliography	101

Preface

Just is: Time, Memory, and Genre

My student-hating, Einstein-looking, lab coat-wearing, tenth grade science teacher blew my mind with his discussions of time. He taught time as a dimension—a fourth dimension. In this dimension, a dimension we can't see, there is no distinction between past and future; there is no time direction. Time just is.

Does that mean only the present exists? Does the past co-exist with now? Or is the concept of "past" a construct meant to explain memory and artifacts? Does the past become real only through the act of narration—a story the memory rehearses and decides upon? Is that story forced into chronological order by narrative expectation? In *One Writer's Beginnings,* Eudora Welty suggests, "The events in our lives happen in a sequence in time, but in their significance to ourselves they find their own order, a timetable not necessarily—perhaps not possibly—chronological. The time as we know it subjectively is often the chronology that stories and novels follow: it is the continuous thread of revelation."[1] Indeed, as we mature, as we construct our life's narration, most of our memories are revelations that continue to unfold in substance and significance.

These morphing memories can be hard to pin down. In addition, psychologists assert we might repress traumatic memories or

---

1. Welty, *One Writer's Beginnings,* 185.

Preface

"borrow" memory content. We may "forget" the image of an act of violence or, conversely, "remember" the suggested tales and sharp details of our photographs: the glistening, gulping rainbow trout we caught as we stood on the rocky shore of Bear Lake; the close-up of our still-round, five-year-old belly covered with chicken-pox spots; and our ballerina poses in blue net tutus and red lipstick. Other artifacts provide clues and corroboration and chronology: a pale wisp of infant hair tied by a tiny white ribbon; boxed Boy Scout badges and WWII medals; yellow, worn written records and newspaper clippings.

We "remember" narratives told and retold to us by family members and friends. These stories are often rehearsed and revisioned at weddings, reunions, and funerals. Author Joan Didion writes: "We tell ourselves stories in order to live. . . . We interpret what we see, select the most workable of the multiple choices. We live entirely . . . by the imposition of a narrative line upon disparate images, by the 'ideas' with which we have learned to freeze the shifting phantasmagoria—which is our actual experience."[2]

The following pages serve as a journal of my remembering, a narration of retrieved phantasmagoric images frozen over time. They are paused, morphed moments mulled for clarity.

This has been a difficult task. Though my science teacher said time "just is," I can hardly find a "just is" when it comes to the revelation and interpretation—and writing—of my life experiences. These remembered moments, many seen first through child-eyes, challenge "voice" and "tense" as I interpret these scenes through an adult lens. These non-fiction, remembered moments about maturation and family string together like snap beads—more like a sonnet cycle of personal essays than an autobiography

---

2. Didion, *We Tell Ourselves Stories in Order to Live*, 11.

1

Refuse

DID MY MOTHER MOAN and turn onto her side in refusal? Did a nurse muffle my cries, cover me quickly like sin, and hasten me away? Slick, bloody, sebum-curded, did I cry for my mother's heartbeat?

Or did my mother embrace me tightly for a moment? Did she kiss my wet face? Did she whisper a tender, forever-message or well-pondered name as she handed me away?

Could I see her face through my swollen, newborn eyes? Did I store the sound of her voice, the feel of her quick-beating heart, and the color of her eyes somewhere in my brain? I want to believe that somewhere in my neural cubby-holes this long-forgotten, flannel-wrapped moment patiently waits to be remembered.

2

Dear Baby Girl

It was late October. I sat on the cold street-curb and waited patiently for the mail to come. I shut my eyes and concentrated, willing that a birthday card or letter would arrive addressed to me. It would start with something like "Dear Baby Girl" and be signed, "Love, Your Mother." I was convinced that someday my birth mother, the one I labored to remember, would think of me on my birthday.

I was adopted by Homer and Melba. After they died—and sometimes while they lived—I prayed for my real mother to find me. "Please," I would beg skyward, "please come rescue me." Even though I was five or six or seven, I still believed hoping could make it so.

Someone told me once that I looked like a young Audrey Hepburn. I savored and mulled the idea, growing it into a happy, secret possibility. One day, probably on my birthday, a chauffeur would drive a black limousine up to my curb. My real mother, Audrey Hepburn, would blossom from the door in a billowing red satin dress and radiant smile. She would embrace me and exclaim, "Baby Girl, I've finally found you!"

Audrey Hepburn never came. Over time my imagining matured, and my tender hopes turned into a sad, secret stone. I realized I must be, instead, a dark memory, a distant, discarded, refused memory. Was my mother raped? Was she a prostitute? Was my father a nameless one-night stand? Did a mere lack of money or opportunity keep her from murdering me in her womb?

Years ago, one sunny afternoon in Salt Lake City, my young daughters and I walked past several panhandlers squatting on the sidewalk near the gates of Temple Square. A thin, pitiful woman in a dirty cotton dress sat spread-legged on the sidewalk. Her graying, unwashed hair was matted from neglect, and her cracked, bare feet were black with disease. She reeked of poverty, filth, and sadness.

Our glances met and I paused. Her eyes looked like mine: hazel, with a brown-gold corona. Her brows arched; her nose was sharp; her forehead high. She didn't look much like Audrey Hepburn, but she did look a lot like me.

3

Anita

HOMER'S WIDOWED MOTHER, ANITA, was a short, round woman who lived alone. She crocheted afghans and pillowcase edges, embroidered days-of-the-week dish cloths, oil painted vibrant green landscapes, and was a good Mormon woman. Her legs were profoundly bowed and, when she walked, she and her black rayon dress swayed rhythmically side to side. Hair nets gathered and tucked in wavy grey-white wisps; thick, seamed stockings gathered and tucked in swollen ankles. She wore tightly laced, black old-lady shoes, and she dusted her age-spotted face with white powder. At home, an ever present, ever clean, starched cotton bib apron protected and brightened her dark house dresses. She and the inside of her tiny brick home smelled clean and sweet like talcum and warm oatmeal.

Melba became violent when she was high on amphetamines and drunk on vodka. I can't remember what set my escape in motion this time, but I knew I had to flee. I ran barefoot through the sleepy morning side-streets of Logan hoping to make it to Grandma Anita's house before Melba could run over me with the car.

A halfway-there gas station slowed Melba down. I darted behind the gas pumps as the car jumped and bounced on and over the curbs. Silently pleading, "Please, please be home," I turned and ran through the middle of the block, racing toward the cement stairs to Grandma's side door.

Grandma Anita hid me in her bedroom. She wedged me between her iron bed and the wall, then positioned herself in the kitchen, waiting behind the latched screen door.

The car jerked to a stop in the street, and Melba was soon confronting Grandma through the screen. Though I couldn't see beyond the safety of the bed's white chenille spread, I knew Grandma was bravely standing her ground as Melba ranted, swore, and pounded on the screen's wooden frame.

Then came a long silence, and I strained to hear the only sound left in the room: rhythmic clicks of a tightly wound alarm clock on the nearby night stand. Curled in my narrow space, I listened and waited.

Minutes later and without words, Grandma pulled me from the side of the bed. We sat for a while, upright, motionless on the edge of the mattress, tears dropping into our laps.

But on a different day of storm and thunder, Grandma Anita held my face in her hands as she spoke. Very gently, almost whispering, she dropped a tiny worm of knowledge into my open, baby-bird mouth: "Homer and Melba had looked for an unwanted, unclaimed baby; money was paid; and your birth-mother walked away from the hospital, alone, without looking back. She didn't want anyone to follow." Grandma felt I should know.

4

Artifacts

On the fourth Monday of every May, I pause in front of a flat-slab headstone carrying a plastic pot of fresh grocery-store chrysanthemums. Green, spring grass hides traces of the long-ago burials. The speckled gray granite is blurred and stained by sun and hard water. The etched dates evidence the time of Homer and Melba's lives.

I was eight and nine when they died. Now, at seventy, I work to image them underneath their small, shared stone: white temple clothes; forever-young bodies tucked tightly in satin upholstered boxes; hands folded; sightless eyes open; faces frozen in expressions of sadness.

I place my solitary flower pot on the granite artifact and water it, hoping the memory it represents will live for another day.

I was bequeathed a cardboard box of discarded, random relics—accidental life-bit artifacts that no one else wanted. Among them were faded certificates, old photographs, and browned newspaper clippings. According to the jigsaw they created, Homer and Melba were living in Cedar City when I was born in Salt Lake. Nested deep in the box was a colorized, studio-picture of a pink baby girl displayed on a shiny satin pillow like a show-and-tell—me, maybe two or three months old. I was wearing a

Artifacts

white, hand-crocheted sweater over a new cotton nightgown. As if startled, my tiny fists were clenched tightly, and my dark eyes were opened wide.

A newspaper clipping showed a young Homer inspecting ROTC troops at the College of Southern Utah. Another photograph showed an apron clad woman bathing that same me-baby in a chipped, white enameled dish pan. Her dark hair was pin-curled and cinched by a bandanna. The woman was young Melba.

I was their only retrieved baby; Melba and Homer couldn't create their own. I remember the long, shiny, vertical scar down the front of Melba's naked body, and I remember Homer's scars, too, both inside and out. All were vestiges of life before me.

5

Daddy

I GLEANED AND PIECED together Homer's World War II experience from the boxed, brown newspaper clippings, a German-censored Red Cross journal, salvaged priesthood meeting "Minutes," a handful of miscellaneous medals, striped and starred bar-ribbon pins, plus sad moments at the kitchen table. Homer didn't speak German or talk much about the war when he was sober, but when drunk, slurred bilingual stories and sobs escaped.

One such night, I couldn't sleep. Melba had passed out on the couch long before, and Homer and I sat alone in the yellow-lit kitchen. Frightened and stilled by his profound sorrow, I focused on the metallic flecks in the white Formica table-top and turquoise, vinyl-covered chrome chairs.

Homer was hunched over, remembering, grieving. He pressed his forehead into his folded arms as he cried, his big man-body shaking with sobs as he revisited past anguish, inhuman brutality, and the guilt of survival.

Suddenly shrapnel exploded into the cockpit of the B-17, ripping open Homer's abdomen and groin. At nearly 30,000 feet above France, as the plane erupted in fire, the crew tried to bail out.

The ball turret gunner struggled forward through the flames and smoke, freed Homer from his seat harness, and pushed him out of the plane through the nose escape hatch.

As Homer's body cleared and his parachute opened, the plane exploded. Homer floated downward, limp, distinctly aware of German troops firing at the remnants of his crew from the ground below.

He hit the dirt, a freshly plowed field, like a dead man. Eyes shut, he waited for the jolt of a rifle blast or the searing penetration of a bayonet. German soldiers, who had commandeered a farmer's grain truck, threw bodies into the back like firewood. Rough hands yanked Homer up and shoved him in, drenching him in the suffocating blood of dead and dying men.

Hunger, cold, and brutality followed. A few prison guards furtively whispered, asking for forgiveness as they carried out cruel orders in the subpens and "coolers" during interrogations at Dulag Luft II and Stalug Luft III. Thirteen L.D.S. men, all Latter-day Saint priesthood holders, found each other—found ways to communicate, pray together, buoy each other up, and find hope. They held "church," telling and retelling Bible, Book of Mormon, and gospel teachings from memory.

As the Great Escape unfolded, they acted as lookouts and carried dirt away from the tunnels. They kept each other safe when 50 other escaping prisoners were murdered by the Gestapo.

The Allied forces were getting closer—the Russians were coming. In the dead of winter, the camp of 10,000 men was ordered to march toward Stalag VII, just outside of Moosberg, 200 miles away. Homer had shoes, but some men, coatless and without boots, walked on rag bound feet in the sub-zero temperatures . . . sheltering in open cattle barns and sheds at night . . . then the boxcars.

Prisoners were loaded into manure and urine fouled boxcars. Packed vertically, they stood arm to arm, back to back, front to front. Some men pressed against the sides facing outward and drew fresh air through open spaces in the dry wood . . . and froze. Those in the center kept warm, but suffocated in the press and the stench or were trampled in animal and human waste.

Snap Beads

The barbed fences of Stalug Luft VII, a camp meant to hold 14,000 French prisoners, soon corralled 130,000 men of all ranks and nationalities. Many men slept in frigid, outside air-raid trenches, sometimes by choice. There, if you didn't freeze, you at least escaped the torture of the lice and rats that infested the barracks.

On April 29, 1945, salvation came: Patton's tanks screeched and screamed, metal on metal, as they plowed into the wired compounds. The man/machine roar of liberation was deafening.

6

Places and Things

As a teller of long-ago childhood experience, I realize I am an unreliable narrator. I want to resurrect Homer and depict him as a grown-up through my own adult lens, but, in truth . . . I never knew him as a man. To me, he was a brief, comforting presence—a warm, sad shade in my space.

Pictures and newspaper clippings depict him as handsome and smart: a real charmer with brown hair, hazel eyes, and a wide winning grin. "Andy," as his friends called him, built glider planes in the family barn and roared through the fields pulling them aloft behind an old Ford pickup. He'd wear his Eagle-Scout badge pinned to his chest, pretending it was Air Corp insignia. He was a shiny-clean, Utah Mormon boy who returned from a LDS mission in Denmark speaking fluent Danish. He founded *The American Farm Youth Journal* at fourteen and became one of the youngest editors of *Boys' Life* magazine and the *Salt Lake Deseret News*.

Homer was a home-town hero who couldn't wait to enlist in the Army of the United States as an aviation cadet.

Later pictures of him—when I was in his world—show a man in his early forties, rounding and balding, with that same Cheshire smile. Besides pictures, I have a few artifacts: a wooden, stenciled desk name-plaque; a chain of dog-tags imprinted with his name, rank, and serial number; a box of ribbons and medals, including a Purple Heart, numerous leaf-crowned pilot wing pins, and his Eagle Scout badge.

I have his pocket-shined, brown leather wallet. There is nothing of monetary value left in the wallet, but oft-handled, finger-soiled biographical cards fill the pockets: his military I.D, pilot and driver's licenses, car insurance and registration documentation, Officer's Club memberships . . . and a laminated Caterpillar Club card, signifying his elite brotherhood with men who have "saved [their] life by parachute." This intimate wallet forever freezes Homer's daily life in time—until the very last moment that he was my father. Sometimes, I pull it out of the box to feel its softness and hold it against me. I know his DNA—silent pieces of him—still live in its worn folds.

Homer was a writer, and I have written remains: His 1929 personal journal of the sea journey to England for the first Boy Scout Jamboree and the bound newspapers he edited for the Washington, D.C., Jamboree in 1937. I have a Red Cross journal filled with "there I was" accounts handwritten by his fellow prisoners-of-war. The stories are strangely dispassionate, almost joking, but the hand-drawn pictures of the camp and the comments about hunger are serious. The men dreamed and wrote about getting home, being with their families, fishing and food. Many of the pages are missing, torn out, censored.

But I do have some memories of my own—most like snapshots, some like movie footage. Because we were often re-stationed after only weeks or months in one place, the memory-time continuum of our life together seems fractured and without sequence. A few memories, however, are hooked to places: the Philippines, Mississippi, Arizona, Texas, and northern Utah.

In the Philippines, though I was very young—maybe four or five years old—I do remember some scary horse-drawn surrey rides with Homer on narrow, misty-mountainside dirt trails. He would sing lyrics from *Oklahoma* as we clip-clopped along: "Chicks and ducks and geese better scurry, when I take you out in the surrey." The drunker he got, the louder he sang.

Places and Things

In Mississippi, when I was in first grade, daddy and I splashed together in the warm-rain street-rivers; we played house in our new Volkswagen camper; we played sweaty house-fort under a giant orange and white parachute draped over the swing set; and we discovered Wonder Bread together. It was here that he taught me when to turn a pancake—when the bubbles pop and stay open on top. In my mind, I can see child-me standing on a kitchen chair with an apron tied up under my armpits, watching dollar-sized pancakes make bubbles.

Arizona breathed hot, dry air and the blowing, shifting sand whispered. I spent a lot of time alone, but sometimes Homer and I would explore. Our chain of base housing, our front door, faced a vast forever-desert. As we tiptoed through rocks, searching for tarantulas and Gila monsters, Apache tear drops and turquoise-in-the-rough, he'd tell haunting stories about Superstition Mountain and the Lost Dutchman.

In Texas, I remember standing on the tarmac in my best Sunday clothes, Homer's large hand holding my small white-gloved fingers. I nearly floated in my buoyant, net-petticoated dress as he stood in charge, bigger-than-life in his pressed dress uniform. The military band played "off we go into the wild blue yonder" as planes flew overhead and hundreds of men stood at attention before us. I could hardly breathe.

7

Mama's Make-up

I REMEMBER SENSORY-HEAVY IMAGES from the Philippine air base: the salty smells and splashing sounds of the ocean; the caws and grunts and chatter of birds, water buffalo, and monkeys; the heavy, sweet scent of orchids; and the oppressive, pungent odor of wet jungle hillsides. I remember standing in our shadow-darkened house behind a screen door with my face almost touching the bellies of giant insects that clung to the other side. Tucked into my bed at night, I'd watch huge, shiny roach-things glint light when they scurried across the floor. The darting, gravity defying feats of our house geckos were startling—especially when they climbed the mosquito net by my bed.

Though still very young, it was here I first noticed Melba as a woman. She wore stylish, netted hats, matching gloves, and high heels. Her linen dresses were tight and bright, and she fully filled them with her Marilyn Monroe figure. Everything was color-coordinated, from her manicured finger- and toenails to her costume jewelry and Merle Norman cosmetics.

Although I wasn't allowed, I liked to touch and smell mama's make-up. There were two special, shiny-gold tubes of eyeshadow. The cases looked like lipstick, except longer and leaner. They twisted up magic missiles of Cinderella blue and fairy-princess purple.

Mama's Make-up

Mama loved lipstick: red, redder, and reddest. These were Scheherazade, Guinevere, Delilah, and Cleopatra colors. Their possibilities made me quiver. I studied how she molded the tips with her lips. Some mothers rubbed their lipsticks down to flat nubs, but my mother applied it like a queen; she artfully created crescent moon-tips with the soft touch of her mouth.

Everything on her dresser smelled like Chanel #5. Rich, heavy, seductive, the cut-glass vial seemed to tremor as it sat, radiating power and calling my name. But I never touched that bottle—I was afraid things, powerful things, would escape like genies from a lamp or spirits from Pandora's box. I didn't want those evil spirits to torment me like they did my mother.

I would sneak into her hot, quiet closet and pull the door shut so no one could see me. Sometimes I'd put her high-heeled shoes on my small feet, but mostly I just wanted to lie there next to a dress or two that I had pulled down from their hangers. The muted light and the lingering scent of her sweet perfume pacified me and helped me love her.

8

The Mustard Seed

I REMEMBER THE SUNSETS of San Antonio. As sunlight faded, Homer and I would lie on our backs in the grass and watch the skies become red, pink, and purple. Dusk—and fireflies—were magical. I caught fireflies in jars with the other officers' children as the skies darkened to black.

Homer would often walk me home from nursery school. Those walks were times of laughter, skipping, and singing. One particular afternoon, Homer became very serious. Even though he was shined and polished in his pressed uniform, he knelt to my level on the gravel road. He opened a small white box that held a glass-encased mustard seed—a pendant orb on a chain.

"Lynn, a mustard seed is like you," he told me. "When it is grown, it is the greatest among herbs; it becomes a tree and birds rest and nest in its branches. If you have mustard seed faith in yourself and in God, you too will move mountains."

Then he kissed my cheek, took my hand, and we slowly, quietly, walked the rest of the way home. I didn't understand the portending significance of this symbolic message and moment—why he was telling me this—but I do remember feeling a powerful, heavy love in my chest.

9

Mississippi

My house was one of many tidy white houses perched politely along a well-tended avenue. Everyone who lived there was white. Everyone in my school was white. Even the stately, heavy-scented magnolia trees that lined the street and garnished our houses blossomed in happy, waxy white blooms.

To the right of my house lived my first best friend, Sally. Sally had two BIG front teeth, scabby knees, and a ponytail. So did I, except teeth—mine were gone. We took dancing lessons together, and our birthdays were one year apart.

We swung from her big-leaf tree in the backyard. A bed pillow-seat was cinched in half by a thick, twisted rope. The rope-knot hurt my bare mosquito-bitten legs and shorts-clad bottom, but the terror of the downswing was worth it. During rainstorms, we waded face-to-sky in our rivered front street and jumped in puddles holding hands. The rain was warm and drenching. It fell in a mixed-idiom of sheets and buckets and cats and dogs.

On late afternoons, Sally, me, and Wonder Bread would sit on the front steps, watching the hot, wet sun go down. I'd carry out the bread bag like a pirate's booty, pull out four or five slices at a time, and squash them together into a gooey bread-ball with my hands.

Sally and I would watch cars go by, listen for the evening crescendo of insect sounds, and slowly nibble the dirt-specked bread balls.

The Mississippi River was also our next door neighbor. Homer loved to fish, and we often had great laughing, watery adventures. Sometimes, though, we would go there to find peace. We'd listen to the life sounds of the great waterway—families playing, birds calling, the swoosh of the current. We'd smell the smells: sweet odors of new plant life and the deep, pungent odors of wet clay and heavy reeds. The air was humid and thick, and it curled my bangs against my forehead.

Though normally a place of comfort, bad things also happened there, like on a certain bright Sunday morning. Homer and Melba had been drinking all night. Melba was in no condition to go fishing—we tried to invite her, but she wouldn't rouse. Homer wasn't sober either; he was just . . . upright. He tried to get the top down on our new white hard-top convertible, but he couldn't manage it.

The high, snaking levee road ran parallel to the river. The water on both sides was deep and murky from recent rainstorms. I nervously watched over my open side window as we nearly missed each curve . . . until we did. As the car began to roll down the levee into the water, Homer swung his arm, knocking me into the leg space under the dashboard. In slow motion, the car submerged right-side up with the hardtop mostly intact. As muddy water gushed into the car, Homer's strong hands found me, pulled me up, and pushed me through his side window. I knew how to swim and, gulping for air, I did. Homer, a big man, forced his way through the window opening behind me.

Drenched and covered with wet dirt, we held each other on the steep embankment. A crowd gathered. The police came.

10

Hide and Seek

MELBA WAS A DRUG addict. She swallowed sedatives to make her sleep at night, stimulants to get her up in the morning, amphetamines to retain her figure, and antidepressants and alcohol to battle her sadness. Some days she zoomed frantically in high gear. Other days, she lay like a dead woman.

Mostly, Melba wanted to die. The methods occurred in alternating streaks: drug overdoses or slit wrists. When Homer was gone, she would go into the bedroom or bathroom to slice herself, locking me out. If Homer was home, she would cut herself, then try to hide while she bled to death.

One particular night of cutting is porch-light clear. I can see our row of base housing—a long row, four apartments connected at the sides. The rows sat back to back. There were no back yards, just narrow, cement and gravel garbage truck alleys. They separated the apartment rows and provided narrow parking spaces by the back doors. Lines of backdoor lights illuminated the alleys at night.

It was a typical hot, quiet Arizona night. Daddy and I were curled together on the couch watching TV in the darkened front room. Melba was in the back bedroom with the light on.

"Peg," he called to her, "come watch with us." He called Melba "Peg" or "Peggy" sometimes. It was his term of endearment borrowed from the first two lines of the song, "Peg O' My Heart": "Peg of my heart, I love you. Don't let us part, I love you."

There was no response. He rose and walked to the bedroom to invite her again. She was gone.

Flipping lights on as he went, he ran through the kitchen toward the back door, yelling "Peg, Peg!" He followed the blood trail leading into the alley. I ran after him sobbing, "Momma, momma."

Not far from my bare feet, a blink of light caught my eye. Melba's cupped, curled hand lay on the ground, her arm extended between two of the neighbor's garbage cans. Her shiny, manicured red fingernails and bright wet blood glistened under the yellow alley lights. Knocking the cans aside, Homer gathered up her near-naked body and carried her back to our apartment. Her escape had failed.

The bleeding stemmed, Homer and I crawled onto the blood stained sheets beside Melba. As the night grew darker, the three of us hugged each other and cried, all for different reasons.

11

Tending Momma

WEEKS LATER, WE WERE headed to Provo's psychiatric hospital in our Volkswagen camper. It was Homer's job to drive; it was my job to tend Melba—to keep her from unlocking the side door and jumping out onto the highway.

She was in a drug-sleep for most of the long trip to Provo, but, as we neared the hospital, she surfaced, shed her pajamas, then realized where we were. When we pulled up to the hospital patient loading zone, she and I were engaged in a frightening battle: I tried to keep her fingers from pulling up the door lock knobs; she fought to push me aside. I was seven years old and no match for her drug-fueled fury.

Melba threw the door open as we neared the hospital curb. She jumped, naked, onto the cement sidewalk, cursing and screaming. Homer sprang from his seat to intercept her. Two male orderlies appeared and the three of them tackled her as she fought, swore, and clawed. A straight-jacket appeared, and the hospital-men bound her as Homer held her down. With sweat and tears dripping down his face, Homer followed the furious battle through the hospital doors and corridors.

Left alone, I crawled back onto a foam mattress in the now-quiet camper and held myself, hoping to stop the sad, beating hurt in my heart. I knew what was next, as Melba did. They would tie her down and shock her, trying to jolt her out of depression and drug dependency. There would be isolation, padded cells, restraints, and the agony of withdrawal.

12

Grandma Leona

MELBA AND I SPENT most of my third grade—and other times off and on—living in a weathered gray-once-white clapboard house with her invalid mother, Leona. Leona was the daughter of a prominent Utah pioneer, L.D.S. bishop, and polygamist. He had seven wives, and Leona's mother had eight children. Leona had 45 other half-siblings. The story goes: Child-Leona discovered she could get attention from her father if she were ill. When a child or wife ailed, he would stop in to visit at that wife's house and bring a token of affection. No one was really sure why Leona was so sickly, but she spent a lot of time in bed.

I avoided Grandma L—she was scary. Except for brown and purple spots, her skin was cellophane see-through. Her white, sparse hair hung in thin, lifeless braids at her shoulders, and her dentures sat in the kitchen cabinet where they fit. Toothless, she mumble-yelled for tea and toast or sometimes warm scalded milk and Lorna Doones. Thankfully, she mostly slept.

Sometimes I would disappear in the overgrown pasture-jungle behind the house that was alive with giant ant hills or crawl under the parlor's never-used dusty dining table to play with my Barbie dolls. The round oak table sat under a window and was tented with a white crocheted, pine-cone patterned tablecloth.

Myriads of miniature sunbeams shone through the cotton lace spaces, turning the floating dust motes into glitter, and lighting the braided rag rug I sat on. Tucked away in privacy, I created an imaginary doll family of happiness.

Sometimes I would play—hide—for hours alone in the dark, very cold/very hot upstairs or search for treasure out in the plastic-sheeted wash porch. There I couldn't hear Leona when she screeched, "Me'ba, Me'ba, Me'ba!" then "'Nette, 'Nette, 'Nette!" if Melba didn't come.

Sometimes, but rarely, I went down into the house's shallow earthen cellar. Steep, narrow, creaky wooden stairs fell downward into a cold, dank, dark hole. Decades old Mason jars filled with brown peaches and pears sat on rickety, failing shelves, and forgotten chunks of black coal still littered the moist dirt floor. The air was heavy and choking with the odor of mice, mold, dirt, and old people. There was a single light bulb hanging from an electrical cord, but I couldn't reach its pull-string. Only a narrow rectangle of light peeked down from the kitchen doorway above. The recesses under the shelves were a blind, night-shadow black, but I knew the mice were there—I could hear them skittering in the darkness.

I could see footprints in the oblong streak of illuminated clay. I wondered who left those ghostlike remains. Maybe they were Leona's frozen-in-time imprints of her younger self or Melba's lonely feet from just yesterday. The shallow overlay of my little tip-toe marks were hardly visible.

I sensed a disturbing kinship and likeness—a sad, codependent marriage between the dying house and Grandma Leona. They had grown old together. They slumbered in tandem, day after day, as silent, barren, bleaching corpses. The mice, Melba, and I, too, shared in this strange symbiotic relationship: We skittered and persisted, living our lives in the unoccupied dark corners.

13

The Gargoyle Upstairs

IN THE SUMMERTIME, GRANDMA Leona's upstairs was oven-hot. I hated having my bangs and long hair stick to my sweaty face and neck, but, there, the solitude was worth it. Sometimes I played alone with my Barbie dolls, but most of the time I explored. There was an endless supply of fascinating things to discover, touch, and imagine. My favorites were The Organ and The Trunk.

An ancient, massive, dark mahogany pump organ sat on the upstairs landing just to the right of the last stair-tread. Surrounded on two sides by the staircase banister, it seemed perched—caged—in an unnatural place. The tall, ornately carved front; tooth-stained, cracked ivory keys; and round, once-white-labeled organ stops gave it a gargoyle appearance. It seemed an aging creature from the past, brooding and gritting its teeth as it peered over the stairs and contemplated its forever confinement . . . alone . . . wanting to sing but forever mute. Its pipes torn . . . its breath gone.

But I loved it. Especially when lonely or afraid, I would sit by my hulking companion for hours, tenderly tracing the beautiful, deeply carved designs with my fingertips. I'd feel every key and pretend I could spell messages to this sweet beast through a musical scale. I'd pump the two, threadbare, tapestry-faced pedals with my small feet, trying to give it breath—but it wouldn't respond. Indeed, our conversations were one-sided.

Perhaps The Organ was The Trunk's sentinel. There was an old, battered oak trunk in the upstairs room where I slept, just around the doorway from the organ. I was NOT supposed to open it, but the trunk was like Pandora's box or Satan's whisper—it called my name.

The lock was beautiful and ornate . . . and open—the key lost long ago. One hot, shadowy afternoon, being completely beguiled, I pulled the trunk-maw wide. It creaked and moaned resistance as it exhaled its dry breath.

The chest was filled with women things—perhaps the remains of Grandma Leona's past hopes or lost dreams. There were yellowed, beautifully tatted, crocheted, and embroidered linens. There were accessories—two flattened, dress-up hats complete with feathers, nets, and hatpins. There was an age-spotted hand-mirror that matched a fancy hairbrush. I perched the hats on my head, pulled the nets over my eyes, and posed like a mysterious beauty into the hand mirror.

But then the horror: The Boxes. There was a string-tied, oblong cardboard box, just the size of a coffin for a dead kitty. I opened the box and gasped—it WAS a dead kitty!

No . . . when I came to my senses, I could see it was a long coiled braid of blond, dead human hair. But knowing that didn't help—it was a real piece of human remains, and I couldn't bear the horror of it. I quickly tightly tied the lid back in place and buried the casket-box deep in the corner of the trunk.

There was another, larger tied box. I calmed down. I waited. I thought about it. Oh, I had to. I cautiously unknotted the string and lifted the lid. Another body! An animal had killed and half-eaten itself!

When I dared pick up the box again and look closer, I realized what was hiding inside: conjoined fur pelts with the heads, tails, and legs still attached. The mink-mouths were trained to wrap around and bite their own tails!

Just as the sunken, shrunken animal-heads repelled me, the long, dark fur asked me to touch. The pelts were soft and horrifically beautiful.

Cautiously, very cautiously, I draped the mink around my neck. I stroked the fur with my hands and picked up the mirror to view my feminine beauty.

I noticed clear, white things. Looking closer, I realized they were dead bug things! Dead moth bodies and molted bug shells were embedded in the hair! Scrambling backwards, I ripped the stole from my neck, flung it back into the trunk, and slammed the lid down.

I didn't open it again.

But the reality of its contents haunted me then and for a long time afterward. Contrasts, parallels . . . how could the horror of it—the beauty of it—relate to the shriveled, barely-living body lying downstairs in her bed?

14

Whiffenpoof

On most winter days, it was too cold to play upstairs. There was no central heating, just a grate over a hole in the upstairs floor. The original pot-bellied, coal parlor stove below had been replaced by a newer version, but the heat still had to radiate upward—to waft up and find its way through the floor-hole. The metal grate kept me from falling through.

Melba and Grandma Leona slept downstairs. I slept upstairs in a cold, terrible-yet-wonderful Alice-in-Wonderland iron bed. It had character. It WAS a character—with history. Its white paint was chipped by the dreams and nightmares of many children before me. Sometimes I fancied myself a new Alice, and the squeaky, snarky metal-coil mattress complained, moaned, and threatened to swallow me every time I moved. It was piled high with worn, hand-pieced kaleidoscopic scrap quilts that continually shed tufts of cotton batting. The mattress and quilts sat so high I had to either take a running leap or climb up the iron frame to flop on top.

The quilts were heavy. If I was tired, the weight pinned me down and swaddled me into a peaceful, womb-like sleep. If I wasn't tired, there was no tossing or turning—I felt like an autumn leaf ironed between two sheets of waxed paper.

Whiffenpoof

When I needed a diversion for sleepless nights. I would drag a quilt off the bed and take position over the warm grate which happened to be located close to The Organ. Light would flood up through the grate, making little square patterns of light on the walls and ceiling and my face. There was a blue, monochromatic picture of a shepherd Jesus on the wall above me. When I tired of my one-way conversation with my mahogany friend, I would talk to Jesus. I knew the parable and song—Melba sang it sometimes: "We're poor little lambs who have lost our way. Bah, bah, bah. We're little black sheep who have gone astray. Bah, bah, bah . . . Lord, have mercy on such as we. Bah, bah, bah."

I knew I was His lamb. I knew He wouldn't lose me. Surely He knew where I was, and that comforted me.

15

Lost

I was ice skating at the outdoor rink in Logan. It was late and time to close; the Christmas carols had stopped playing. The overhead lights had blinked off, making it hard to see, but I could tell our car was gone. I skated over to the outside edge of the ice and crunched awkwardly through the crusted snow to the empty parking space. The car, our black Rambler, was gone; my shoes, inside, were gone. Homer was gone.

I stumbled back to the ice and started to slowly skate around the perimeter. The sky was clear. The white moon and stars softly lit the night, making the frost on the ice and trees sparkle in navy blue. There was a vacuum of sound. The other skaters had left, and I was alone. Only an occasional car swooshed past, interrupting the blue stillness. My pace increased as my resolution grew. I wasn't lost; Homer was lost. If I started to walk home, maybe I would find him along the way. Even though I was very cold—my face, hands, and feet were burning numb—I could do it. I dug in the front teeth of my skates, my new white pre-Christmas skates that Homer had given me a few days before, and pointed myself in the direction of Wellsville, fifteen miles away.

The shadows grew blacker as I shuffle-skated through the streets of Logan, and the cold penetrated. My frozen feet and ankles became unruly with numbness and fatigue, and I was beginning to hear noises. A sputtering engine slowly approached me from behind, and I peeked up as it passed. A shadow's gaze met mine. The shape turned back to the wheel, and the dark car turned the corner in front of me. I chop-stepped faster and told myself not to be afraid.

Within minutes, I heard the car coming up behind me again. It stopped. I froze. A hoar-frosted window whispered as it sunk into the car door. "Little girl, it's dark and late. Get in and I'll give you a ride."

"No thank you," I whispered back with my eyes shut. Homer had told me that little girls shouldn't get in cars with strangers. "My dad is lost. When I find him, he'll take me home."

"Where do you live?"

"Wellsville."

The dark door swung open. "Get in," the man commanded.

I wanted to run, but my trembling legs and frozen feet failed me. I got in. Although my mittened hand clutched the door handle tightly, another part of me sighed with relief.

As we pulled up to the street-lighted front of the police station, my mixed feelings intensified.

"Sit still," the man instructed and slid out of the car. I was ready to run now, but my thoughts stopped mid-flight when I realized I was staring into the back window of our black Rambler.

A dark uniformed figure, a policemen, bent down and opened the driver's door. He smiled and whispered, "Come with me; *I'll* take you home." His strong hands pulled me across the seat.

"I think your dad's in the drunk tank. I'll take you both home."

16

White's Motel

HOMER RETIRED FROM THE Air Force; his years of flying and being important ended. We were living in White's Motel, a short train of little kitchenette rooms that ran parallel to the Logan River and Main Street. It must have been summer; it was warm and I wasn't in school. Both Melba and Homer were drinking heavily, and Melba was mixing her alcohol with drugs. The fridge was empty except for a few bottles of beer, and the tiny, fold-out kitchen table was littered with half-full bottles of vodka and dirty ashtrays.

Melba was usually on the bed, sprawled in her underwear, drug/alcohol-sleeping. Homer sat in the one bigger chair, watched television, slept, and drank. We didn't go fishing anymore.

Once in a while, Homer and I would walk to the store to buy a few groceries. He still liked to make pancakes, but most of the time I was hungry. Usually, a jar of peanut butter sat on the table, but there was rarely any bread.

A big, shaggy stray dog often hung around the motel looking for food scraps. It occurred to me that we looked a lot alike—long brown matted hair and round brownish eyes. I sat on the cement outside the screen door of our motel room and lured him with peanut butter. We'd take turns: I let him lick the spoon, then I'd lick the spoon. As long as I gave him peanut butter, he would stay by me and let me pretend he was my dog.

One morning, Homer and Melba didn't stir. I watched TV for a while, then wandered around the parking lot outside, playing with rocks and keeping an eye out for my adopted brown dog. When it got closer to midday, I went back inside, hoping Homer was awake. But . . . something was very wrong. Homer had rolled, pulling the sheets with him. He was wedged between the mattress and the wall. He wasn't the right color—sort of yellow-purple—and it scared me. I jumped on the bed and tried to wake him. I shouted "Daddy!" and pulled on his heavy arm. His flesh was cold. I had never touched a dead person before, but even in my innocence, I knew he was dead. I moved to Melba and shook her, yelling as loud as I dared.

She was insensible, but warm.

I went back outside and walked around the parking lot, wondering if I was supposed to tell. The only other people I sort-of knew were the managers, a young husband and wife who lived in the main office apartment.

I stood for a while with my toes touching the bottom of the office's two, crumbling cement stairs. The front door was open, but the inside was dark. I reached up and knocked on the wooden screen. I knocked hesitantly, then harder. The screen door hung slightly ajar, and it banged into the frame with each knock. The wife slowly emerged from the shadows, cradling a fussing baby in her arms. She looked annoyed.

"I need help," I blurted. "My dad is dead and my mother won't wake up." I shook. My child-voice trembled. I waited, looking up at her.

She was silent for a moment. Then without opening the screen, she berated me from the shadows, "That is the worst thing I have ever heard! Why would you tell such an awful lie?"

Disgusted, she turned away and disappeared, leaving me standing there.

I didn't know what to do. I turned, walked slowly toward our motel room and sat down on the hot cement by our open door. I waited . . . for something, anything . . . maybe for Jesus. In a while, quite a while, the manager-husband walked from the office toward me. I braced; I assumed he was coming to scold me, too. Instead, he walked past me without a word and entered our apartment. In minutes, he threw the screen door open and ran back to the office.

I waited. Before long, two police cars drove into the parking lot. Once again, the officers walked past me without speaking—like I was a bystander who didn't belong there. I got up and followed them in.

One officer hovered over Homer, the other shook and jolted Melba until she roused. He tried to talk to her, but she was incoherent and had to be held upright. I heard the screaming of an ambulance getting louder and knew it was coming for us.

I watched Homer's big body bounce on the gurney as they angled him through our doorway, rolled him to the ambulance, and pulled-pushed-lifted him inside. I wanted to yell "Wait!" but I couldn't find my voice—or myself. Homer was gone and, in the commotion, I was lost, too.

I don't remember who came to claim me, but I know it wasn't my mother.

17

Too-ra-loo-ra-loo-ral

I BELIEVE MELBA WAS overjoyed to adopt a baby. She told me once that, out of all the babies in the world, she chose me. She said she loved me and, later, promised she wouldn't drink anymore . . . because she loved me.

One year for my birthday, she crocheted a pair of yarn poodles, one pink and one white, with pom-pom ear tips and shiny button eyes. They were loose covers that slipped over empty whisky bottles. As we washed out two bottles and covered them with the crocheted poodle bodies, Melba held me close and whispered, "This is their only use. I won't drink anymore. I promise." We perched the pretend puppies on my tall bedroom dresser by the doorway. "But remember," she admonished, "these are just to look at, not to touch."

I promised.

She liked to sing, and I melted when she sang lullabies. I remember her gently holding me on her lap when she was sober and whispering, "Too-ra-loo-ra-loo-ral , too-ra-loo-ra-li, hush, little baby, hush now, don't you cry. Too-ra-loo-ra-loo-ral , too-ra-loo-ra-li. . . ."

On one such night, a few months after Homer died, Melba hugged me as I climbed into bed. She began to sing:

"Too-ra-loo-ra-loo-ral. . . ." As I listened with my heart, I looked toward the open door where the hall light shone onto my dresser. The glass bottles glistened beneath the yarn. They were now half-full.

18

Hair

PAJAMA CLAD AND BAREFOOT, I stood inside the open fridge door. I grabbed the heavy, silver pitcher with both hands and took a big gulp of the orange juice. I could smell and taste the vodka, but, besides a couple of frozen Milky Way candy bars, there wasn't anything else in the fridge. I quietly placed the cold metal pitcher back inside and softly closed the door. I could hear Melba banging around in the bathroom.

I stood outside the bathroom for a while, watching as she struggled with the sharp hair scissors. Melba just couldn't get the angle right to cut her own bangs. Then she noticed me.

"Your hair needs cut, " she slurred. "It hangs in your face."

I knew a haircut at that moment would not have a good outcome. I shook my head and inched backwards into the hallway.

"Come here!" she shouted. "Come here now!" She tried to follow but was too drunk, too drugged, too unsteady to catch me.

When she stumbled around the corner into the front room, I saw her grip on the scissors had changed. She was fisting them tightly with the closed tips pointed downward. In that instant, I knew with certainty that she would stab me.

I bolted out the front of our apartment, ran across the street and banged on the nearest neighbor's door. Thankfully, the neighbor-lady was home and she let me in. She shut and locked the door behind us and called the police.

19

Suicide

AFTER HOMER DIED, MELBA'S suicide attempts intensified—usually drug overdoses now—and things spiraled downward quickly. Melba rarely left her bedroom and was non-responsive most of the time. She rented an apartment in Roy until we were thrown out. Then, we stayed in a little house in Layton. Here I realized my mother and I were not like everyone else.

When not in school, I lived in almost complete isolation and played alone. I spent hours costumed in dress-ups or Melba's clothes, drawing and coloring, reading books, and playing Barbies. I would dress our real poodle, Suzette, in doll clothes and pretend she was my baby or little sister.

I asked the neighbor-girls over to play, but their moms always said no. Cathy, who lived just a couple of houses down, told me I smelled dirty like booze and cigarettes. Cathy was clean and shiny and smelled like lotion. She had a mom and a dad and several brothers and sisters, and they all ate dinner together in their dining room. They took piano lessons and went on vacations. They went to Sacrament Meeting, Sunday School, and Primary. Her mom said she couldn't be my friend at her house, my house, or at school.

Snap Beads

I got up whenever I woke up, looked for food, and put on whatever dirty dress was still on the floor, usually my brown gingham one—my favorite. Sometimes I had anklet socks to wear, sometimes I didn't. I tried, but I couldn't quite manage putting my uncut hair into ponytails or braids. I did comb it—sort of—but I wasn't very faithful in finding shampoo or taking baths. I walked to school and I walked home. I often went to sleep in front of the television at night and generally slept on the floor or the couch. During the week, I ate school lunch when I could find money in Melba's wallet or when someone secretly paid. (I knew it was my teacher.) On the weekends, I would take my scavenged coins to the local hamburger drive-in to buy onion rings or to the corner market to buy my favorite treat: silver-ball cupcake sprinkles.

There were a few brief moments when things seemed right. Melba started attending Alcoholics Anonymous meetings and found a boyfriend, Merle, at the AA meetings. He was a nice man with a broken life who lived alone over the bowling alley in Brigham City. There was a span of a few weeks when Melba got up in the morning, combed my hair, made me take baths and brush my teeth, bought and cooked food, and cleaned the house. Melba played the role of mother, and I played the role of child. I was happy, and I thought she was, too.

Then early one morning, I woke abruptly. I heard the fractured sounds of broken dishes and tipped kitchen chairs. I found Melba hunched over the sink, hardly able to stand or talk. Her slurred, drooled words sounded like, "Help me, Lynette."

My chest felt like stone. Just days before—good, happy days—Melba promised again that she wouldn't cut herself, drink, or take pills anymore . . . because she loved me.

"I hate you," I spit out, trying to sound cruel. "You promised! If you loved me, you wouldn't do this!"

I stormed to my room and dressed. Avoiding the kitchen, I found Merle's phone number, called him to come, then ran the entire three blocks to school.

At the end of the school day, when I started down the sidewalk toward home, I could see several cars parked in front of the house.

Suicide

Immediately, I knew—I had already imagined and rehearsed this moment many times over in my head. I knew Melba had finally gotten her wish.

I hesitated. Where could I go? School was the only safe place I knew, but the door would soon be locked. Melba had no friends, and the neighbors pulled their blinds against us. I had no place to hide, no place to pretend this wasn't happening.

I took baby steps. I walked in circles. I sat on the curb. Finally, I stood outside the door. It was quiet inside—dead quiet. Everyone inside was waiting for me.

I hushed the door open in slow motion. Merle and Melba's brother and sisters were sitting in a circle in the front room. For a few seconds, no one spoke—they just looked at me with sad, droopy eyes and faces. Merle approached, got down on one knee, tried to hug me, and said, "Lynette, your mother has died." Again, the room was silent. Everyone expected me to cry, so I did, then I walked to my bedroom, softly shut the door behind me, and sat on my bed, waiting.

I had always been alone, but I had the security of an apartment or house or bedroom or car—some place to attach to when all around me shook and stormed. This was a new version of alone. As the reality of my situation sank in, I began to cry in earnest—not for my mother, but for myself.

20

Things

"I want the Gold Bond stamps—you can have the S&H greens."

"I want the mahogany carved salad set from the Philippines."

"My daughter can fit into Melba's dresses and shoes. I'll take them. Who gets the perfume and jewelry?"

"I guess we throw away Homer's old uniforms. No one wants those."

"Does anybody need the car—or should we sell it?"

"Let's make a list of how to divide up the furniture. There isn't much of value—except Lynette's new white bed. My daughter would like that."

"And the dog. Do we drop it off at the pound?"

I sat outside and listened and watched Melba's family throw her life and the remains of Homer's into trucks and garbage cans. And my life. The artifacts, the evidence of our three lives were now reduced to unwanted refuse.

I could hear the whimpering and yelping sounds of my sweet dog-baby, Suzette, coming from one of the cars. I wanted to throw myself on the ground and scream "mine, mine!" but I had no voice—I couldn't save us or our things. I couldn't save Suzette. I sat on the curb, crying deep inside, watching cars and trucks drive away with the fragments of all we were.

Things

Now, I wasn't the prettiest baby in the hospital; this time no one wanted to take me home. Would I be left on the curb like our furniture? Was there a pound for unwanted children?

21

Maybe

The poet, Sylvia Plath, committed suicide the same year my mother did. Earlier, in her journals, Plath had recorded her wish to die and tried to explain why, writing, "I desire the things that will destroy me in the end."[1]

But Melba didn't write it down or tell us why. That secret of why hurt deeply. I thought Homer and I were her best friends, the only people who tried to love her, the only people to tell. It felt like rejection or betrayal or punishment. Sometimes I would talk to the sky and ask Jesus why Melba would do this to Homer and to me—and why she would do this to herself.

She was two people. There was Melba, a wife and mother, who cheerfully surfaced some days, put on her make-up and fixed her hair. She would make us shrimp cocktail, Homer's favorite, as if nothing terrible had happened the night before. She'd smile and hug us when we told her how good her food-gift tasted. Sometimes after a suicide attempt, she would tell us she loved us and apologize like she knew how it broke our hearts.

At other times, we didn't exist. All that existed was her desire to destroy herself—to go, to escape, to die.

---

1. Kukil, *Unabridged Journal of Sylvia Plath*, 63.

Maybe

I wondered if her unhappiness and need to leave was my fault. I thought, maybe, if I were a better child, then she would have wanted to stay and be my mother.

But I didn't have the understanding or capacity to save her—I was only nine, and she was already lost.

When did that happen? When did she slip away? Where was Melba all those years when Homer was in the spotlight? As a new bride when Homer went off to war, what did she do? When he was shot down and "missing in action," when she thought he was dead and her life stood still, what then? When Homer came home from the war a deeply changed and hurt man, how did she adapt? Is this when she started to drink—to find a way to connect with Homer's world of night terrors?

Homer was restationed over and over again, well before Melba could make friends with the other wives or join a club or get a job. How did she fill her days or become important? Was the drug addiction a fatal response to her need to have value, to be beautiful or productive—or to escape her own deep isolation and loneliness? Did she ever long to tell me, her child-companion, of her loneliness and hurt? Maybe those rocking, softly whispered lullabies meant more than I knew. Maybe they were really for her.

Unlike Homer or Sylvia Plath, there were no journals, newspaper clippings, pictures, writings, card-filled wallets—or babies who looked just like her. Besides a few pictures, just four artifacts remain of Melba: a shared, Homer/Melba headstone, an incomplete set of Noritake china that I never saw her use; a soft blue, cashmere cardigan; and the diamond wedding ring the mortician slipped from her finger as he shut the lid on her coffin. Otherwise, her entire human essence and the deep sadness of her life exist only in a tightly tied box in my memory. When I die, no one will be left to remember that she lived.

22

A Heavy Stone

A WILL WAS FOUND. A few things were allotted, as was I. I was bequeathed to Melba's nephew, an up-and-coming young Air Force officer stationed in Washington.

Kneeling backwards with my chin resting on my crossed arms, I peered over the back of the couch . . . watching through the front window . . . looking for someone I didn't know to drive up to the curb. This wouldn't be Audrey Hepburn or the real mother I had long hoped for; this would be a stranger who was coming to take me away. I had no child words, nor do I have the right adult words to describe how I felt: hope . . . fear . . . loneliness.

Homesickness. Maybe, that was it. I was homesick, aching for a place that didn't exist.

I don't know if Homer and Melba asked permission first—I assume so—but the designated guardian-couple, Michael and Susan, must have been stunned. They already had a young son and daughter, and Susan was heavily pregnant with another baby. I certainly wasn't the child they were expecting.

Though I was basically obedient as children go, I'm sure I was a challenge, a precocious intrusion, a very unexpected and unwanted long-term guest.

A Heavy Stone

And I wasn't like other children. I was used to being alone—of not interacting or bonding with other people. I had already learned to watch the world with detached emotion, growing a heavy stone heart to ground and protect me.

23

Covenants

HOMER AND MELBA HAD been baptized and confirmed. They had received The Holy Ghost and been married for time and eternity in the Logan LDS temple. They were part of the Mormon heritage and culture, but, like distracted sheep, they strayed and were lost.

When I turned eight, the age of accountability, I too was baptized and confirmed. My Aunt Alda—the wife of Melba's brother—saw to that.

Usually baptism is a wonderful family event. Parents and Primary church leaders prepare eight-year-old children by helping them learn and understand the Church's "Articles of Faith" and the concepts of baptism and repentance. Fathers baptize and confirm their children, blessing them with the companionship and protection of the Holy Ghost. Family and friends are invited to attend both the baptism and confirmation services. It is a warm and joyous occasion, a day of celebration.

My baptism was a planned kidnapping of sorts. I put on a dress and stood just inside Grandma Leona's front door. The long glass window in the front wooden door was covered with a see-through, once-white gauze curtain that smelled like dust. I pressed my nose against it and watched for Aunt Alda to drive up. I was nervous, hoping no one would notice I was gone.

Covenants

Alda took me to the Hyrum Stake Center church house. A random, young priesthood holder was assigned to baptize me. I don't remember much about the baptismal font or the immersion, but I do remember worrying that I now, officially, promised Jesus and my Heavenly Father that I would forever be good.

Aunt Alda helped me dry and dress. I didn't want to look too wet or guilty when I was dropped off back at Grandma Leona's house.

The next Fast Sunday, Alda's husband, Uncle Dan, placed his hands on my head, confirmed upon me the gift of the Holy Ghost, and blessed me as a new official member of the Church of Jesus Christ of Latter-day Saints.

24

Families are Forever

SEALING IS IMPORTANT IN the LDS Church. "Without the sealing power, no family ties would exist in the eternities, and indeed the family of man would have been left in eternity with neither root [ancestors] nor branch [descendants]. Inasmuch as . . . a sealed, united, celestially saved family of God is the ultimate purpose of mortality, any failure here would have been a curse indeed, rendering the entire plan of salvation utterly wasted."[2]

Aunt Alda and Uncle Dan made sure I was sealed by proxy to Homer and Melba in the Logan LDS temple. I wasn't born "under the covenant." Homer and Melba had been married and sealed together in the temple where they were promised an eternal family if they lived righteously. Their natural-born children would have been born automatically under that covenant. But I was an adopted post-add-on.

Homer and Melba broke the promises they had made in the temple. I couldn't be sealed to them when they were here on earth because, in their sinful state, they wouldn't be issued a recommend to re-enter the temple for the sealing ordinance. The hope was that they had repented and were obedient in heaven, and that now, by proxy, the sealing was appropriate.

2. Holland, *Christ and the New Covenant*, 297–298.

Families are Forever

Much of that remembered experience is a fuzzy, white montage: the whiteness of the Logan temple, the white clothing of the temple workers and patrons, and the whiteness of my borrowed, cotton sealing dress and slippers.

I understood the basic whys of this sealing, but not the details. What if the sealing didn't work because Homer and Melba were not following Jesus in heaven? Might I still be an orphan there? That did seem likely. But, perhaps, maybe, my real birthmother and father would be obedient. Maybe they would finally find me in heaven.

25

Spin the Bottle

Jeffery, my very first boyfriend, was in my 5th grade school class, plus he lived just through the block on the Air Force base in Spokane. He was cute, funny, and smart. He had a sparkling smile and bright eyes; he was clean and shiny.

After I was taken in by Michael and Susan, I became a strac trooper, too, like Jeffery. My hair was cut short, and my clothes were clean. I now smelled like soap; Jeffery smelled like soap. We both had short hair that stuck up. It was a match.

In the summer and on warm weekends, we would skateboard together. Skateboards—then skinny short boards with fixed rollerskate-type wheels—had just become a fad. They didn't steer well at all, but it was possible to build up some dangerous and thrilling speed. Because the streets were mostly flat, we would tie jump ropes to the back of our bikes and tow each other behind. The tricky part was knowing when to let go.

The friend-crush Jeffery and I had for each other was just progressing past the road-rash stage when Michael was restationed, and we had to move from Spokane to Prattville, just outside of Montgomery, Alabama. Prattville, pronounced "Praat-vull," wasn't like Air Force neighborhoods where kids moved in and out regularly. Prattville was off-base, and a newcomer there was big news.

Spin the Bottle

I was a novelty at school. Kids would group around me, trying to get me to talk. They said I had a hysterical accent. I, on the other hand, couldn't understand half of what they said, and I never did figure out where "over yonder" was or the distinction between "ya'll" and "all ya'll."

Not long after we moved in, I was invited to a birthday party. It was for Thomas, a boy at school who had been staring at me and sending me flirtatious notes. I had been staring at him, too: He had creamy olive skin and a cute turned up nose. The party was at his house and most of our school class was invited. I bought him a present, put on my Sunday dress, and Susan dropped me off at his house.

The minute I walked in, I wanted to bolt. A Beetles song was booming from the record player and kids dressed in hip-huggers and colored-lens granny glasses were lying around on pillows or dancing. After some really awkward moments and intense stares, however, they seemed to accept me. I guess they assumed my dress was just a weird mid-western or Mormon thing.

Then it was game time, and the parents were nowhere to be found. A glass Coke bottle was produced, and the rules for "spin the bottle" were explained. We were all to take turns spinning the bottle on its side. The spinner-person and the person it pointed to were supposed to go into the bedroom located right off the front room and kiss. When they re-entered the room, everyone was to cheer and applaud.

I was in a dead panic.

It was Thomas' turn. He announced that since he was the birthday boy, he could have several turns. He kept spinning the bottle until it landed on me. Everyone cheered and laughed, and Thomas held out his hand to take me to the bedroom. Even though I wanted to run, I laughed, too, and tried to look like this was something I did all the time.

He led me to the dark bedroom and grinned at the crowd as he shut the door behind us. He walked quietly toward the back of the room and beckoned me to come closer. Trying not to trip in the darkness, I haltingly moved his direction. He met me halfway, put his hands on my shoulders and pulled me toward him.

This was it—the moment I had dreamed about: My First Kiss. And I was petrified. Just as Thomas leaned in to kiss me on the lips, I bent my head down. He kissed me on the forehead—maybe for a lack of alternatives. But he smiled, picked up my hand, and led me back to the door.

When the door flew open, everyone cheered, and Thomas and I laughed. My failure was our forever secret.

26

Segregation

PRATTVILLE WAS A TIME and place of physical maturation and a broadening social understanding. It was also the time of the Civil Rights Act of 1964, and Governor George C. Wallace's refusal to integrate schools. It was a place of "White Only" signs posted on the restaurants, motels, public restrooms, and public drinking fountains. It was a time when I witnessed white crosses burning in yards and frightening KKK demonstrations.

I attended Prattville Junior High off-base. One morning before the first bell rang, large, polished black cars drove up to the front of my segregated, all-white junior high school. Four big black men—called Negroes then-—and one black girl, about my size, emerged and walked straight to the principal's office. Immediately the whole school was electrified with curiosity and a foreboding sense of danger.

The next day the same convoy, plus a few police officers, arrived. It was obvious that this black girl was trying to enroll in our all-white school. Adult employees were furious, and teachers refused to accept her as a student. She sat in the library with her bodyguards and pretended to read, never looking up or acknowledging the white faces of children pressed flat against the library windows.

Snap Beads

She didn't end up in my classes, and she didn't eat in the lunchroom. I only saw her in the halls between bells. There, every 45 minutes, a horde of white students parted, and she walked the gauntlet.

A couple of days after she enrolled, I was walking down the hallway with my friends just after the first bell rang. I heard jeering, and I looked up to see her coming my way. She walked silently and deliberately, staring down at the floor, alone in a crowd of people. Kids started to layer three-deep against the walls and yell insults.

"Nigger, you don't belong here!"

"Get back where you belong, nappy head!"

"Awwww, Nigger cooties!"

Boys ran up and poked her with their fingers, then acted like they were dying because she was diseased or had cooties. Finally, one boy pushed her hard, and her tightly clutched books fell and skidded across the floor. Kids squealed with delight and cheered as she stooped to gather them. No teacher intervened—they watched from their classroom doors.

And I stood there, frozen. I was from the north and none of this made sense to me. I knew I should have helped her—even just to pick up her scattered pencils and paper. But I didn't. My fear of a major, middle school faux pas was stronger than my desire to do what was right.

She was gone within the week.

27

Residential "School"

WHAT DID MICHAEL AND Susan say? How did they tell me I was to leave, that they no longer wanted me in their house? I don't remember. I just know I was about thirteen, old enough for most boarding institutions to accept me and old enough to be sent away. Me and a little blue trunk filled with a few belongings, hopes, fears, and plenty of sadness were left at The Misses Howard's School for "select young ladies" in Birmingham, Alabama.

The school was straight out of the movies. The "campus" sat on a hill overlooking the city and consisted of two massive, white antebellum-type plantation houses. The estate's orchards, farmland, and pastures had been sold off to developers long ago. Giant oak trees served as sentinels while kudzu choked out the azaleas and dogbane that grew below. A few long blades of grass struggled to live under the massive shade trees, but, facing the street, the lawn on the front hillside was neatly groomed for effect.

The houses were aged hulking ghosts of an earlier grand era. The public lower floors showcased chandeliers, oak paneled walls and floors, and massive oak staircases. Now the wood, worn smooth to a dark, ghostly patina, evidenced the hands and feet of hundreds of girls who had walked the halls, floors, and stairs.

We were allowed to entertain guests in the parlor of the main house, although the worn brocade settees were less than entertaining. An intimidating, grand piano separated the sitting room and the formal dining room. Here many "select young ladies," including me, labored over the keys. The piano, too, was well-worn, with chipped ivory keys and gouges in the black, once high-gloss finish.

A dimly lit, tightly spiraled servant/student staircase climbed vertically from the kitchen recesses of both houses to the sleeping quarters and classrooms above. Although the woodwork was dark, everything else was a dingy white: the walls were a dirty plaster-white; our bedding was bleached yellow-white; and our bed frames were chipped, hospital-white metal. We kept our few possessions, bits and pieces of our prior lives, locked in our small trunks at the foot of our beds.

In my house, the main house, there were about eight beds crowded into the upstairs big bedroom. A huge, claw-footed tub lay belly-open in the one bathroom we shared. Though sitting on vicious feet, its open cradle-womb became our nursemaid: Miss Bonnie, the headmistress, sent us there to soak if/when we had "uncontrolled emotions." It worked. The warm amniotic water soothed us as we floated and cried in curled fetal positions.

Only three adults slept in downstairs bedrooms. Miss Bonnie and Madame Gublou lived in the other house; Miss Pearl, Bonnie's sister, lived in the main house—my house. Willie, the main house butler, simply disappeared at night.

Madame Gublou taught French so we would become cultured and refined. She was kind and pleasant—and blind. Completely blind. Miss Bonnie provided room and board in exchange for French lessons.

Willie was known to us as a "negro" who was "retarded." He was small, bent over, and he grumbled under his breath as he shuffle-stepped around in a starched white uniform. Though his uniform was tended to, the sisters, Miss Bonnie and Miss Pearl, hadn't helped him with his teeth. He had a couple of yellow ones left that were hard to look at when he grinned. It wasn't a friendly grin. It was a sinister I'm-going-to-kill-you-in-your-sleep smirk.

Residential "School"

We had dreams about him crawling out of the attic or cellar or crawl-space at night to REALLY kill us in our sleep.

Miss Bonnie and Miss Pearl were spinsters, proper white-haired southern belles, rigid relics of a past time and culture. Well ... Miss Bonnie was proper, but Miss Pearl was in the process of losing her mind and her inhibitions. She had outrageous bursts of hysteria and should have spent time in the tub.

The two were opposites in other ways: Miss Bonnie, the sister in charge, was tiny, birdlike, neatly tucked in, and intense. She always seemed to be in a focused hurry; her whole body leaned forward before the rest of her followed. She still played the piano beautifully, and we often heard her haunting, classical music late at night.

Miss Pearl was a large, big-boned woman with a wild look about her. She loved to watch "professional" wrestling on a little black-and-white television in her downstairs bedroom. When the rest of the house was silent, we could hear her shouting brutal "Kill 'em!" rants of encouragement.

Miss Bonnie and Miss Pearl did have one thing in common: They fiercely protected their distance and separation from us. We lived in their houses, but we were not allowed to enter their secret worlds.

We boarders were a motley lot. There were only a couple of us who were real orphans. A few parents sent their daughters there to protect them from having to be with "coloreds" in public settings. Other girls were sent there because of bad behavior or pregnancy. Boarding didn't make bad behavior stop, however. These were the early 60s, and drugs, especially marijuana, were passed around and experimented with. My house boarded the younger girls; the older girls stayed above Miss Bonnie. Over there, a person could get high from just breathing the air.

And there were boys—boys who didn't come to sit on the settees. I was young, 7th or 8th grade by then, and still believed I should be good. This naughty world of misbehavior was nerve-wracking, and I wanted to leave.

28

Howey Academy

My trunk and I were sent to Howey Academy, a larger boarding institution in Florida, just outside of Orlando. It was a true business and things ran like clockwork. There was a headmaster, a counselor, secretaries, teachers, maintenance workers, live-in "dorm mothers," a stainless steel cafeteria, and regular cinder block classrooms.

Some students came during the day, but fifty-or-so girls and boys lived there. Adult-wise, all but the dorm room mothers and a small crew of employees went home after the school day ended. Then, the prefect system kicked in. A prefect supervision and disciplinary system, patterned after English monastery boarding schools, assigned older students policing and disciplinary powers and responsibilities.

I wore a uniform during the day—a navy blazer with the Howey Academy insignia on the right breast pocket, a white collared blouse, a knee-length navy pleated skirt, navy or white socks, and saddle shoes or loafers.

There was a resident Catholic priest—the Vice Headmaster—who literally took care of vice and conducted mass on Sunday mornings and vespers on Wednesday nights. We were required to attend, appearing in a hat or head-covering on Sundays. Being

LDS, mass and vespers seemed strange and confusing. I had a hard time knowing when to stand or sit or kneel, when to "intercede" with choral responses, and Latin was totally beyond me.

Stereotypically tall, dour, and dressed in black, the priest drifted in and out of our daily existence: He was an ever-present shadow in the dorms, the dining hall, and in our required nightly study sessions. He made me feel nervous and guilty, and I tried to avoid eye contact.

The palm-dotted land around the school was sandy. In the back, it sloped into a murky lake, where water snakes and alligators watched for us. This was a place of creatures. The sand was full of chiggers and mites; large black cockroaches ran over and around us at night; and, when in season, we found little green frogs in our shoes and underwear drawers in the mornings.

There was a pecking order in dorm room assignments. I had five roommates in my first room. We were all newcomers to the school and younger than many of the other girls. Our room was located on the same end of the hall as the dorm mother's apartment. Each of us was allotted a bunk bed, a four-drawer clothes chest, space for our trunk, and half a closet. The community shower down the hall provided us with a crash course in social negotiation, adaptation, anatomy, humility, and public shaming.

After I had been there a while, I was promoted to prefect rank—probably because of my continued determination to be good. I was moved down to the opposite end of the hall into a smaller room and assigned one roommate. She was a Catholic from Brazil, and she was one tough, big girl. She hardly talked—although she sometimes mumbled in Portuguese—and we had little in common. I don't believe we ever had a meaningful conversation either before or after "that day."

As a prefect, it was my job to assist the dorm mother, help needy students, and enforce law and order, especially inside the dorms. When there was a rule infraction, I administered a "stick." Our sticks were modern-day symbolic versions of the corporal punishments that prefects of old administered. Thankfully, I didn't have to hit anyone with a cricket bat or hockey stick. Instead, I turned in paperwork to the administration, and they assigned service hours: cafeteria work, yard work, facility cleanup, etc.

There was a small group of "rough" girls on our hall who bullied others and made life miserable. One, a brawny, broad-shouldered girl, was particularly mean. The night before, I had given the leader of this group—that girl—a stick for being cruel to some younger girls on our hall.

Classes had just ended, and I was alone in my room. I had climbed up on my top bunk and was absorbed in my homework. I heard movement and, just as I looked up, my nemesis, the mean girl, grabbed my ankle with a jerk.

Instinct caused me to start kicking. As she tried to drag me off the top bunk, I rolled and clung to the mattress and bed frame. The harder I kicked, the harder she pulled, twisted, and fisted my legs and back with her knuckles. I knew that either she was going to make it up onto my bed—using me as the ladder—or she would succeed in yanking me to the ground.

Suddenly my roommate appeared in the doorway. She grabbed the girl by her hair and pulled her backward, nearly jerking me off the bed, too. Once on the floor, my roommate hit her in the face and dragged her out of the room. Abruptly as it began, the fighting stopped, and it was silent—except for my own panting. I pressed myself back against the wall and pulled my legs up, hugging them tightly. I waited for a return. Nothing.

A couple of hours after the attack, I cautiously ventured into the cafeteria for something to eat. My roommate was there, sitting with her Brazilian friends. She didn't look at me; she didn't speak to me. She acted like nothing had happened.

There was no sign of the mean girl or any of her minions at the tables. The next day the school cancelled the bully's enrollment contract, and she disappeared.

29

Finding Peace

ALTHOUGH RADICALLY DIFFERENT FROM Misses Howards' School, Howey Academy was also movie worthy.

Even with that overlay of "safe" adult structure, we still created an underlying world for ourselves—a world in which we took care of each other. We created our own families. We had our own sets of rules, operating procedures, and hierarchies of influence. The older boarders mothered and raised the younger ones.

The school sat in the middle of quiet, misty orange and grapefruit groves. Though they were privately owned and off-limits, they called to us. When our small dorm rooms and social orders became too hard to bear, we would head there alone to walk through the trees.

Depending on the time of year, we could listen to the soft sounds of insects, frogs, and birds, and smell the citrus scent of the trees and the richness of the moist earth and humid air. We often ran into each other sitting, walking, or running through the trees, escaping loneliness and sadness in our own ways. For me, this quiet place of solitude was where I went to be alone. Here I spoke to the sky, hoping Heavenly Father and Jesus could hear me. I wanted to be safe. I wanted to be loved. I wanted my real mother and father—and my Heavenly Father—to know I existed and that I was still waiting to be found.

Lucky boarders could fly home for Thanksgiving, Christmas, and summer break. For those who weren't lucky, on the day before breaks we would watch quietly from doorways and windows as students with families were cheerfully loaded into airport taxis and private vehicles.

Christmastime was the hardest, even though the school made an effort to celebrate. There was a tree in the dorm commons area, and Christmas carols were played on radios and record players. The cafeteria served turkey and dressing. The room mothers took us into town the week before so we could buy little trinkets to exchange. At night, we would gather in the commons in our pajamas and try to be cheerful for each other. We'd sing and exchange happy family memories, then return to our dark, empty rooms.

30

Heavenly Father, Are You Really There?

I HAD BEEN DROPPED off at an Orlando medical clinic so I could get a prescription for antibiotics. I had strep throat. The school van was late to retrieve me, and the clinic closed while I waited on the step. I stood there shivering and burning with fever as the streets darkened and a heavy rain began to fall.

Orlando was a dangerous place at night for a lone young girl. As people of the streets began to step from the shadows, I pressed myself tighter into the clinic door's recess. I felt so miserable and so alone—and so afraid. Those feelings weren't new, but this time, sick with fever, I felt true despair.

I turned my tears skyward into the rain and poured my heart out. "Please, Heavenly Father," I begged, "please see me. Please find me."

At the end of my lament, my pleading, I felt calm. The van quietly emerged from the darkness and pulled up to the curb.

A couple of days later I received a letter. Because receiving mail was such a rare event, I knew before I opened it that something significant was about to happen.

Snap Beads

The letter was from Aunt Alda. It was brief, saying only that God had impressed upon her that I was to come stay with them in Utah for a while, maybe until I graduated from high school. All I had to do was go to church and act like I liked it. I was thrilled by the offer, and her request seemed reasonable. I had worked at being good for a long time. I knew I could become the good Mormon girl Aunt Alda hoped for.

31

Wellsville

WHEN I WAS LITTLE and staying at Grandma Leona's house, I spent a lot of bike-time on the secret sidewalk. The secret sidewalk stretched east-west across a green pasture, rode the old train bed, and bridge-spanned the shallow creek. Only people who spent slow summer afternoons on horses or bikes knew it was there.

Standing where the cement started, I had envied how its grayness reached straight and focused—it knew where it was going. The cement was old, not light, but dark gray and sprinkled with chips of embedded quartz that glittered in the sun. Shallow drawn lines, barely a finger-tip deep and wide, divided the cement into tidy 3'x3' squares.

Now, I was back. I laid cheek-down on a clean square above the creek, arms and legs straight and relaxed, palms resting on the hot, rough concrete. Fingers spread, my senses of touch and smell thawed and focused. My empty self absorbed the mothering heat, the insect-sound lullabies, and the soothing swoosh of the water below. The bitter, musty odor of horse dung, the minty tang of watercress, and the sweet smell of warm pasture grass lulled me. I shut my eyes and felt my heart beat softly in my chest. I was home. I knew I belonged here.

Snap Beads

Aunt Alda and Uncle Dan were generous and kind. They offered board and room without complaint, even though they were retired, aging, and their income was meager. There were no rolled eyes, sarcastic remarks, or paused conversations. They acted like they liked me. We all understood this living arrangement was temporary, however. I had until I graduated high school.

32

Paul McCartney Eyes

I WAS SITTING IN Sacrament Meeting with Aunt Alda and Uncle Dan. There was a young man positioned by the pulpit who had just returned from his two-year, LDS church mission. As per general operating procedure, he was to report his experience.

It was the summer before 11th grade. I was sixteen and still in love with the Beetles, particularly Paul McCartney. The young man rose, and there at the pulpit stood Paul's look-alike. I don't remember much of what he said; I was too busy looking at his dark McCartney eyes.

And, yes, his name was Paul! His family belonged to our church ward, so now our paths crossed every Sunday. I was intent on attracting his attention, but I was almost five years younger, and that made it harder to be in the same places at the same times. I was a young high school student; he was a college student. Looking at each other during Sacrament Meeting and passing in the church halls just wasn't enough productive exposure.

One late Saturday morning, I was spread out on a blanket in the grass beside Aunt Alda's house. I was working on tanning my front side. I was greased up with baby oil and my little white two-piece tanning-suit was wet with sweat. My mascara-smeared raccoon eyes and messy hair were evidence that I had just gotten

Snap Beads

out of bed. I was listening to my little transistor radio and trying to drift back to sleep—until I felt a shadow.

I opened my eyes and looked up into Paul's face. This kind of exposure wasn't what I'd had in mind.

"Hey, do you want to go into Logan and get a drink at Pete's Spudnut?" he asked.

After stammering something affirmative, I jumped up, grabbed the blanket for cover, and ran into the house leaving him standing there. I had no time for makeup, but I quickly rubbed my blackened eyes clean and ran a brush through my hair. I tried to wipe off excess baby oil, squirted myself with too much of Aunt Alda's Emeraude cologne, then pulled on some Levi cut-offs and a light cotton shirt. I grabbed some sandals and stumbled out the door. When I turned the corner of the house, Paul was waiting, leaning against his new red GTO. He opened my door, and I slid in. Literally. I noticed how shiny I was making the black naugahyde bucket seat.

I rolled my window down so the wind would blow my hair—all the way into Logan—so I would look wind-blown, not bed-headed.

We gave our order to the carhop. She returned in a few minutes and hung our tray on the driver's side window. I was slowly gaining composure and self-confidence as we chatted and sipped our sodas.

Until . . . I realized my drink was leaking into the crotch of my pants and onto the now-greasy black seat. I wanted to go home at this point.

After Paul dropped me off at Alda's, I felt sick. I had blown my chance. I drew warm bathwater, hoping to wash away the morning's baby oil, sweat, and my own stupidity. As I started to undress, I realized the zipper was down on my cut-offs and probably had been all morning.

33

Christmas 1970

It was Christmas 1970. Paul and I drove to Salt Lake City to walk through Temple Square and enjoy the beauty of the Christmas light display. As always, it was beautiful and very cold. Nearly every bush and tree on the square was lit—illuminated and sparkling—in beautiful Christmas colors and patterns. Frozen ice and snow crystals glistened in response, as did the temple's gray granite and the tabernacle's aluminum dome.

Inside the visitor center's rotunda, the majestic, eleven foot statue of Christ, Thorvaldsen's Christus, stood below a heavenly ceiling mural of stars. Christ's arms reached out, and the inscription at the marble base beckoned, "Come unto me, all ye that labor and are heavy laden, and I will give you rest." Paul took my hand as we looked upward and stood in emotional awe.

It was late as we dashed to find our parked car in the cold darkness of the Salt Lake night. Inside, the car's heater worked to take away the chill, and we hugged for warmth in the blinking shadows of the frosted windows.

Paul fumbled in his pocket. "I couldn't think of what to get you for Christmas, so maybe this is okay," he whispered as he produced a small ring box. "Will you marry me?"

34

Becoming a Wife

PAUL AND I MARRIED the April of my senior year. Although we planned our honeymoon around my high school's spring vacation days, Aunt Alda still had to excuse me from school for my temple endowment and wedding.

It was a sharp and clear spring morning; the Logan temple grounds were budding with the symbolic promise of a new beginning. During my endowment session, I sat in beautiful new temple clothes and was taught about Christ's Plan of Happiness and Salvation—about my responsibilities and potential blessings. As my head spun in overload, Paul and I knelt, facing each other at the sealing altar. Holding each other's hands, we were married "for time and all Eternity."

Having never talked to anyone about birds, bees, or birth control, I immediately became pregnant. I was very thankful that my body would look "normal" until after I graduated from high school. Meanwhile, my friends were being called in by the high school counselors. They talked about colleges, scholarships, and vocations. No one called me in.

On my graduation night, I drove myself to the high school and found my new alphabetic chair position. I sat there on the bright stage during the ceremony and watched the crowd of adoring parents taking pictures of their graduating children. At that moment, I desperately wanted a parent to be there for me—to point and say they were proud. I looked upward toward the stage lights to keep tears from falling onto my cheeks and graduation robe. In the bright haze above, I thought I saw someone—a spirit-image staring down at me. Was it Homer or Melba? Was it my real mother? Or, maybe, was it Jesus or the Holy Ghost? Or . . . maybe I imagined it.

When my tassel was shifted and the ceremony was over, I sneaked out the back of the stage to avoid the hugging, picture-taking families and ran through the darkly lit parking lot. I slipped into my car and locked the doors. I sat there for a while, watching families and loud, celebrating seniors drive away. A very familiar loneliness settled upon me as I drove home in the dark.

I parked outside our newly rented studio apartment and turned off the car lights. After a few minutes of tearful solitude, I dried my face, put on a smile, and went inside to be a good wife.

35

Snap Beads

"Don't put them in your mouth. You'll choke," I was admonished many times as a little girl and for good reason: I lo-v-v-v-ed my pastel plastic snap beads . . . cradled in my mouth, plugged inside my ears, or hanging around my wrist and neck. Alone, each was smooth, shiny and felt good on my tongue—like a candy. But its potential was better: By holding hands, by snapping together, they became beautiful necklaces. They belonged; they fit like a family of pearls. They fit like I wanted to fit.

It was time to start my own necklace. It began with Paul, then Tiffany, Tauna, and Tara were born. Finally, Tayson came along to begin the strand.

Our second home was a mouse-ridden, small pink camping trailer plopped in the middle of a barnyard. It was far cheaper than the studio apartment; Paul milked the cows to pay rent. Thankfully there was no room for furniture, for we had none.

This camper was our sweet, new baby Tiffany's first home. There was a small, three-foot long Formica table top that folded up and down in the kitchen area. We put a little portable crib in that space and thereafter ate on metal, folding TV trays. It was fortunate that Tiffany was a tiny thing, too, and that space seemed made just for her. She had a pug nose, wispy, brown hair, and colic.

Snap Beads

She cried and cried... and cried. Paul and I spent many days and nights bouncing her on our knees, hoping she could feel better and go to sleep—hoping WE could feel better and go to sleep.

We didn't stay there long. The war in Viet Nam churned and dragged, and Paul knew he would be drafted. Soon after Tiffany was born, Paul enlisted in the Army. He, Private Riggs, was assigned to an infantry division and soon left us for basic training at Fort Ord, California.

Three months later, we all headed for Fort Carson, Colorado.

Here, we lived in a trailer again—this time, thankfully, in a trailer park, not a barnyard.

Near the end of his service, we returned to Wellsville where baby #2, Tauna, was born. She was a beautiful baby with a headful of black curly hair. She was very funny and rarely cried. I had recurring nightmares that I hadn't fed Tauna for weeks—that I had lost track of her completely because she was so quiet. Eventually, I'd find her dead and withered in her bassinet. In reality, she was always eating and far too plump to wither away. While Tiffany rejected her food, Tauna ate everything in sight.

Two years later, baby daughter #3, Tara, arrived. Tara was our only blue-eyed, fair-ish child. Her wispy light brown hair grew into long, thick, amazingly beautiful curls. Tiffany tended and mothered her sweetly; Tauna wasn't quite sure about this new sister—she was competition.

Almost eight years after Tara's birth, our son, Tayson, arrived. None of the sisters were quite sure about him. Tayson was a round-eyed, round-faced little boy who delighted in driving them crazy.

As I carried these babies in my womb and met them for the first time as newborns, I thought of my birth mother. I loved my sweet babies, and I marveled at the miracle of their births. How could my mother not want to love me as I grew inside her, as our hearts beat in tandem, as she labored in childbirth and first gazed into my swollen, newborn face? I wasn't just confused and hurt, I was angry.

During ancient Roman times, unwanted infants were abandoned to the elements and left to die. The babies who survived abandonment were up for grabs. If someone wanted a child, they could search the pile and take one. I saw the parallel: I was abandoned to fate, and Homer and Melba picked me up. It was incomprehensible to me that my own birth-mother had left me on that pile of abandoned babies.

36

Sunrise, Sunset, and So Forth

THAT STRANGE CHEMISTRY TEACHER from the past also talked about our ebb-and-flow perception of time. One possible explanation of the perceived variance, he explained, was that time seems to speed up because adulthood is accompanied with fewer and fewer memorable or first events—a first kiss, first day of school, first job, first death. Routine makes time seem to go faster.

As an adult, I once tried to keep a diary. My monotonous entries could fit almost any day: I woke up, showered, dressed, put on makeup and fixed my hair, fixed breakfast, woke and fed everyone else, cleaned-up the kitchen, helped the kids get ready for school, tried to do family prayer, rushed out the door—Paul to work, me to work, the kids to school or the babysitter. Then I worked, worked, worked, ran errands on the way home, took kids to after-school sports or activities, picked them up, fixed dinner, cleaned the kitchen and dishes, completed church responsibilities, facilitated homework, got the kids in the tub, made sure everyone's clothes were cleaned, mended and ready for the next day, said bedtime prayers, read stories in bed, tucked everyone in, talked just to my husband, cleaned up the house and did last-minute chores (laundry, sweeping, wiping), watched the news, read the newspaper, and fell face first into bed in complete exhaustion. The days flew so fast I couldn't fit everything in, including journal writing.

37

New Year's Eve

BUT WEDGED INTO THAT fast-forward living were moments when life did stand still. One cold, snowy New Year's Eve is frozen in my mind forever.

Our nephew was getting married that night—at midnight—and we were dressing to attend the ceremony. Paul and Tayson had headed down the highway to our pasture below the house to do last minute, before-bath chores. Standing in the bed of the pick-up, Tayson was preparing to cut bales and pitch-fork hay.

Tara and I, back at the house, began to hear sirens, and we walked to the back glass doors to see what was happening. Below us, by the entrance to our pasture, our farm truck sat askew on the shoulder of the road. A stranger's car had settled into the barrow pit another hundred feet down the fence line.

An ambulance pulled up, blocking our view of the truck. Instantly and with few words, Tara and I struggled to get our boots and coats on as we charged through the back doors and leaped from the deck into the deep snow on the hillside. Taking giant, stumbling strides downward, we neared the bottom just as a line of people—EMTs, neighbors, and strangers—lined up to stop us from getting closer. We could see Tayson being loaded onto a gurney, while Paul, dazed and battered, stood in the snow. The ambulance quickly headed for Logan with lights flashing and sirens screaming.

We waited outside of the emergency room while they worked to stabilize Tayson. Soon, a young intern entered the waiting room and sat beside us. Bent forward, elbows on knees, head in his hands, he told us the situation was dire. Tayson might not live. He had a massive concave skull fracture; his brain was traumatically, critically injured. His femur was shattered; his collarbone was snapped; his lung was shredded by blunt force. Barbed-wire fencing had carved deep lacerations in Tayson's head, sides and back. He needed to be flown to Salt Lake City.

We had only moments to be with him before they loaded him onto the Life Flight helicopter. Gathered Priesthood holders anointed Tayson with oil; their hands were laid on his head, and he was given a Priesthood blessing. Not knowing if he would survive the flight—if we would see him alive again—Paul and I kissed Tayson's swollen face and his motionless, closed eyes.

He was bound for Primary Children's Hospital. Paul and I stood in the darkness, holding each other . . . feeling indescribable despair. We watched the helicopter disappear into the night sky, and we silently prayed for Tayson's life with united, focused intensity.

Our Bishop was waiting in his car to drive us to Salt Lake, over an hour away. Our farmer-neighbors converged to feed the cows.

Paul had heard Tayson knock on the cab's back window as they pulled into the entrance of the pasture. He didn't realize Tayson was trying to tell him a car was speeding down the highway toward them. The driver was asleep, and she was headed for the bed of the truck like a guided missile.

When the truck stopped spinning, Paul jumped out, looking for Tayson. He searched the wild, tangled hedge by the road, but he wasn't there. He spotted Tayson's lone boot lying about 50 feet out into the pasture. Frantic, looking north toward the other car, he saw Tayson's body hanging in the fence, his skull crushed, his leg freakishly positioned. Paul ran to him, freed him from the

New Year's Eve

barbed-wire, and laid him in the snow. Kneeling next to him, Paul cupped Tayson's head, knowing that, somehow, he had to stop the blood. A young man, a stranger, suddenly appeared from behind with a clean, flannel baby blanket in hand. Other drivers had also witnessed the initial impact and Tayson's catapult into the roadside poles and fences. They had stopped at nearby houses and called 911.

The car ride to Salt Lake was an eternity long, and we had no idea if Tayson had survived the flight. When we arrived at the hospital, Tayson was still alive, and the surgeons were already teamed to begin. When they removed the top quarter of Tayson's fractured skull they found that the thick, meningeal tissue encasing his brain was badly traumatized, but miraculously intact.

Our family and friends moved with us to the intensive care waiting area to watch for Tayson to emerge from the operating room. Still lingering there, a man, woman, and two teenagers slowly prepared to leave. They were a rough bunch and, judging by their appearance, life had already been hard. The nurses had just removed the body of their dead son from the very bed that was being prepared for Tayson. The teenage boy had swallowed battery acid to punish his parents for a perceived injustice.

The family was alone and grieving. As we entered the small waiting room, they paused only one moment more, then slowly gathered their things and left. In our own deep sorrow, we watched their sorrow. I wept for me, and I wept for them. I wondered if this was the bed where another young boy would die that night—my own.

38

The Hour of Lead

—Emily Dickinson

ONE DARK, WINTER NIGHT as I sat alone with Tayson in his hospital room, I wrote, wanting to capture his valor in suffering and record his redemption. Though my heart was broken and the scene hideously surreal, I wanted to remember what might be our last time together:

"My always-active son is still—his boyish, nail-chewed hands, his forever-dirty knees, his heavily-lashed dark eyes. Only his chest bucks with the gasps of the respirator he's tethered to. The yellow line on the screen overhead jerks in agony and anger. A tear forms at the corner of his jellied, unblinking, half-open eye. I touch his tightly swollen, corpse-cold index finger, hoping he can feel I am here, hoping he can feel how deeply, desperately I love him."

"Tayson, can you hear me?" I whispered aloud, choking back my own sobs.

"A clear balloon full of blood and spinal fluid dangles from the top of his smashed skull. Brown bile darkens the drainage tube in his abdomen; the urine bag fills; the respirator sighs; the chest tube

The Hour of Lead

protruding from his side sucks bloody, cloudy fluid from his shredded lung. Red saliva bubbles on the sides of his taped mouth. His little-boy stomach trembles and this chest pulses shallow breaths between the heaves of the respirator. His broken shoulder moans in purple, green, and yellow. His shattered femur hasn't been reconstructed—it is stretched out and tied straight on the sheets. A cord connects his foot to a weight that dangles from the foot of the bed."

"I love you, Tayson," I mumbled, my lips pressed against his wet cheek.

I knew if Tayson did survive, he might exist only as a living body. I wondered if I should pray for him to live . . . or pray for him to die.

Tayson was first in a coma, then an induced coma so he would remain motionless. Death would be easy; he was already standing beside his Heavenly Father. Just one silent step more, and Tayson would be in God's arms. Tayson's body was in that bed, but his spirit, his true self, was already patiently sitting like a good little boy in the waiting room of heaven.

The nurses attended Tayson tenderly: They spoke sweetly to him, read to him, and played music. They, too, silently prayed for him and handled him like he was their own. I hung Tayson's recent 5th grade school picture on the brain pressure monitor above him. I wanted the nurses to know what Tayson looked like and who he was—the bright, hazel-eyed, handsome boy who loved sports and mischief. But as I sat by his bed and watched him struggle to live, he slowly became another person.

39

Before And After

When Tayson was medically allowed to surface, to wake, when he first opened his eyes, we wept in happiness and sorrow. Most of his body was there, but "Tayson" wasn't.

By then, metal rods protruded from the flesh of his thigh, and an outside "fixator" held his femur together. The upper right quarter of his skull was missing, and a thin layer of skin that covered that section of his brain pulsed with his heartbeat. His beautiful eyes were vacant and unfocused.

He was a newborn in a boy's body. He didn't remember how to suck from a straw or swallow food from a spoon—he was fed through his nose. He couldn't sit up, talk, walk, or show emotion. The nursing staff would tie Tayson upright in his wheelchair and see that he got "out and about" rides for stimulation.

One day, Tayson's best friend came to visit him, and the hospital staff suggested they play video games. Tayson was tied into his chair and handed an Atari controller. Though he wasn't looking at the television screen, he held the Joy Stick and moved it side-to-side like he had done so many times before the accident. This was an amazing, unexpected breakthrough.

Paul and I tag-teamed between the hospital in Salt Lake and home. We both had to keep our jobs and our insurance. In our absence, Tara held the world we knew together. She was in high school—getting herself up every day, getting her homework done, doing her laundry, buying groceries and making her own meals. Tauna came home to help; Tiffany, now married, supported; and, often, the Relief Society women brought meals to the house. Priesthood men took care of the animals.

Though the Tayson we finally brought home from the hospital was now a stranger, he saw himself as the same fifth grade boy who had gone down to feed the cows. He had been good at sports, especially baseball, and he wanted to play again. Paul and I thought hard about this. If he were hit in the head by a ball or bat, it would probably kill him. His running was different, his decisions were very different, his batting couldn't happen at all. We had to decide when/how we should let him re-enter the world of other boys.

One bright, warm day, I was sitting behind the baseball team bench, thinking how glad I was that Tayson had progressed enough to be tolerated there. The other boys were kind, but the coach didn't put Tayson in to play outfield or infield—Tayson just wore the uniform and sat on the bench.

During a calm moment, the coach and his assistant, both fathers of boys on the team, sat down in front of me within hearing range. The assistant complained about the parents who pressed him to play their boys more. The other, the coach, replied, "Yeah, you have to deserve to play on this team."

40

Fire!

It was Valentine's Day, and I had just returned home from Pocatello where I was completing some coursework at ISU. I pulled into the garage, parked, and walked toward the back door of the house.

My senses leaped—something was terribly wrong. The window in the back door was black, blackened on the inside by a swirling mass of frantic, ashen particles. And the scream. I could hear the house—the fire alarms-—screaming inside. I stepped up and touched the door with my fingertips. The house was pulsing, heaving to catch its breath.

Ignoring all I had been taught about fires, I threw the door open and ran inside. Surely I could throw out or extinguish whatever was burning. Even though I couldn't see flames, the air was dense, black, and caustic. I grabbed the house cell phone hanging five feet inside, pivoted, and lunged back through the door.

Just as I cleared the doorframe, a ball of fire exploded horizontally through the house, throwing me into the snow at the bottom of the steps. Windows shattered and doors flew open.

I lay there stunned. Though I still gripped the phone, I struggled to dial 911. I was shaking too hard for my fingers to find the numbers.

Fire!

Later, after Wellsville's volunteer fire department had finished their work and all was dark and quiet, I stood at the back end of the house where the girls' room had been and looked out into the cold winter night. Framed by open, gaping walls, the moon shone and the sky was alive with bright stars. The frosted landscape was strangely peaceful, beautiful, and unaffected.

The choking chemical stench kept me grounded, however. The air was unbreathable, and I pulled my shirt over my nose and mouth trying to strain out the still-floating ashes of my life. The moonlight and night-shadows outlined a few remains. Like a charred ribcage, blackened, partial spindles of the Porta-Crib I had raised my babies in jutted upward in silhouette out of the nearby snowbank. Burned blue-pink-black remnants of my daughters' prom dresses, now covered with ice, lay near the crib.

The enormity . . . the gravity of the situation was incomprehensible. It was past midnight, and we had no place to sleep or find warmth. There were no pajamas . . . no toothbrushes . . . no food. I looked upward at the clear, starry sky and prayed to my Heavenly Father for a place to sleep and a way to feed my family.

And I gave thanks. I could have been burned or killed. Paul and Tauna had been at work; Tara and Tayson had been at school; Tiff was at her house. We were safe. Our house was destroyed, but everything that mattered was intact. We had each other.

Immediately, Paul's family, our friends and neighbors, and our church ward stepped forward with offerings of shelter, clothing, food. . . .

41

Finding My Mother

I HELD A WISTFUL dream, a game of hope that slept secretly, quietly, in my adult heart: Did my mother live nearby? Was she a secret neighbor or friend? When I noticed a resemblance—hazel eyes, a sharp nose—I'd silently wonder: Are you my mother? Are you my father? Are you my sister? Brother?

Not long after I became a new mother, I sent my name and how-to-find-me information to the Utah Adoption Register. If birth-parents were looking for their child, they could use that data pool for information. As a refused child, however, I had no right to initiate a connection.

Years passed. My mother must not have known about the resource, I reasoned. Surely if she had, she would want to find and know me. But she didn't, and in my heart I knew the truth of it.

As I entered grandmotherhood, I decided I must finally act; I had stood on the curb and waited long enough. My mother and father would soon be too old to find.

Though forever hurt and angry, I knew I could pull this box of sadness off my psychological shelf and untie it. At that same time, Ancestry.com, Progeneologists, and DNA testing became accessible. I submitted a saliva sample to Ancestry.com, then contacted a researcher at Progeneologists. The researcher helped me petition the state of Utah to open my birth records—to untie the box.

Months passed, but information finally started to surface and connect. A judge in Cedar City helped me access my original birth certificate and adoption records. Those original records identified Judy Green as my mother, who was living in Salt Lake City when I was born. No father was recorded. There was also an interesting X-ed square on the document: Judy had already given birth to a baby boy two years prior. She marked that this baby was dead.

I now had a direction. Through online research, I discovered that Judy, now in her 80s, was still alive and residing in Salt Lake City. Two years after my birth and pregnant again, she had married a Salt Lake doctor and given birth to the first of another five children.

She was from southern Utah, and brothers, their wives, nieces, nephews, and cousins were still there and connected on Facebook. When I contacted them, also through Facebook, news spread like wildfire, and they began contacting me. They shared pictures and information about Judy and the Green family.

And they shared a knowledge of the baby boy. A few years before, there had been a similar connection made by two young women, Hanna and Heidi, who were living in Idaho. They were the daughters of that supposedly dead baby boy. He, my half-brother, was now really dead. He had committed suicide—shot himself in the head with a shotgun—when the girls were young children. In his belongings and papers they had found adoption records that led them to Judy and the Greens. When approached, Judy turned her back and told Hanna and Heidi, her first sweet grandchildren, to go away and never contact her again—the birth certificates and adoption papers were lies.

42

Another Lie

JUDY WAS LIVING IN an assisted-care facility. She had suffered an aortic aneurysm and mild stroke earlier in her seventies, and now, in her eighties, she needed extra physical support.

Her pregnancy and my birth were probably nothing more than miserable, complicating nine-month-long social inconveniences. To me, however, she was an imagined presence that had haunted me my entire life: I had wished for her, dreamed of and imagined her, loved her and despised her.

But in my sixties, any naive, pretty dreams of her acceptance had long ago dissipated. What remained was, simply, the desire to know who I am and where I came from. Then, finally, I could fit. I would be legitimate—a real snap-bead in a greater whole, a real line on a pedigree chart.

Being the second, secret dead baby from the past, I knew my existence would be stunning—not to Judy, but to her children, my existing five half-brothers and sisters. I knew I needed to proceed gently. I didn't want to cause a family war or jeopardize Judy's health by just appearing, so I first sent a letter and a self-addressed envelope. She didn't respond. I then sent a letter to her son, my half-brother. I hoped he would be kind.

Another Lie

He took my letter to Judy, who told him it was another filthy lie: I didn't exist like her first baby boy didn't exist. She was certain of that. She'd X-ed us both out of existence on hospital records.

My new-found half-brother wrote back, telling me to go away—to never contact any of them again.

43

Another Story

THIS WAS JUDY'S MOMENT: a time of reckoning; an opportunity to set pride and deceit aside. With only a bit of lifetime left to set things right, she refused.

She died a couple of years later. We never met.

I also wrote the oldest daughter of Judy's five children, Lorraine, whose birth followed mine by two years. She, too, submitted her DNA to Ancestry.com. It matched.

Lorraine helped me know Judy further through stories and photographs. One picture, taken in the assisted-living home, was recent and mesmerizing. Judy was smiling and looking directly into the camera. Her hazel eyes were dark and wide, and her expression was defiant. Her hair was very much like mine—naturally curly, short—just grayer. Her smile was engaging, surly: The ends of her mouth curled like she was thinking of something sarcastic to say. Oddly, I felt a strange softening after all these years of furiously hating her. I could tell she had grit—like I do. Maybe that is what she gave me; maybe that is my umbilical inheritance.

Together, Lorraine and I worked to figure out who my father was. At her own emotional expense, she took tied, sad boxes of childhood memories off her own shelf to help me.

Another Story

Memory pieces slowly melded into a narrative. Lorraine remembered standing at the foot of a gravesite while Judy cried over the headstone of a man called "Hal." She remembered seeing a small, framed picture of someone she didn't know—a young man—hidden in her childhood home. Judy told Lorraine it was a picture of Hal, a boyfriend from the past.

Both Lorraine and I worked to pull information from the Internet. Nothing solidified until it suddenly did: a close connection, a first cousin's DNA results on Ancestry.com. He did NOT connect to Lorraine—he was not her cousin. He was NOT related to Judy. Immediately we started combing through online obituaries in order to trace backward from this cousin. His father or mother would have to be a brother or sister to my father.

Yes. His uncle went by the name "Hal."

A story pieced together, The Williams family ran a successful swing band in the 1940s and 50s. Hal was the drummer. Dark and handsome, always wearing a grin, he was a social magnet—and married.

Hal's wife discovered his infidelity. There was a near-divorce, but Hal's family, his wife and three children, ultimately held together. Judy, spurned, left for Salt Lake City to find a job and wait out gestation. I was born a few months later.

Jerome Bruner writes: "Through narrative, we construct, reconstruct, in some ways reinvent yesterday and tomorrow. Memory and imagination fuse in the process."[3] The narrative of Judy and Hal emerged and evolved, founded on printed artifacts, online sources, and a convergence of family memories. There are huge gaps and a lack of humanity in this construction and reinvention process, but I believe these stripped down, fractured life-pieces contain basic truth.

---

3. Bruner, *Making Stories*, 93.

44

Graveside Services #1 and #2

When Judy died, I hoped that maybe I could sneak into her funeral service and see her in her coffin. It could be my only chance to look at her, to gaze into her face, to talk to her, and, perhaps, to touch her. I wouldn't speak to anyone else. I'd just slip in and out like a ghost—the ghost she deemed me to be.

But there was just a family graveside service planned, one far too intimate for a ghostly visit, and the casket would be closed. Besides, really, I didn't want to ruin those last memories for my siblings. I could only imagine how ugly the confrontation would have been if they had recognized me—a sister who wasn't supposed to exist.

Lorraine died a few years later. Instead of a typical viewing and burial, she wished to be cremated. Though the ceremony was to be simple, brief, I imagined a larger crowd would gather—she had many friends who loved her. I loved her, too, and that gave me the courage to quietly pay my last respects.

It didn't turn out like I had planned; there was no subtlety. Lorraine's husband, a kind man who had supported our tandem family research efforts, felt it was important to meet my/her brother and sisters—Lorraine wanted that.

Graveside Services #1 and #2

   As he introduced me, I was met with fierce stares and stony silence. Their disgust and hate was palpable. After glaring at me for a few minutes, after making sure that I was punished by their repugnance, they turned their backs to me in collective, symbolic rejection and abandonment, then walked away without a word.

   Other than embarrassment, I felt little emotion. I already knew the outcome of this long-anticipated meeting and didn't expect anything else. Indeed, this was a foreseen burial of my old hopes of familial reconciliation and acceptance.

45

Graveside Service #3

I WAS SURPRISED WHEN a lifetime-ago cousin, the daughter of Homer's much younger brother, found me. She let me know her mother had died, and they were going to travel here to bury her locally. I was invited to the graveside service.

The cemetery was snow-shrouded and cold the day of the burial. As my husband and I made our way toward the warming tent, I felt uneasy. I intended to stand quietly along the perimeters of the crowd so, perhaps, no one would notice me. Many years had passed since I belonged.

The ceremony was a sweet celebration of a good woman's life. Family members came forward and recounted memories, recreating her life and their relationships to each other through stories. As I listened and watched, I began to notice faces turned in my direction. I was being noticed.

Following the closing remarks, dedication of the grave, a final "amen," and an emotional, unison group pause, people I didn't recognize began to gather around me and introduce—reintroduce—themselves. They were long-ago cousins. We exchanged phone numbers, emails, addresses . . . and hugs . . . like a family.

46

Trunk #3

Anticipating that I would be there, one cousin brought an artifact, a gift: Homer's military travel trunk—large and cumbersome—that had been patiently waiting in a basement for over 60 years. What an amazing, unexpected gift! My mind exploded with thoughts of the potential contents, and I couldn't wait to get it home.

The trunk and I sat on the kitchen floor. Though dirty and well-worn, I knew there must be something significant inside. Maybe this trunk would be like Grandma Leona's, filled with saved importance, relics of the past, and fragments of hope and joy. Or . . . maybe this was a traveling box of sadness, too big to tie with a ribbon and place on a shelf. Perhaps, maybe, it was the symbolic predecessor of my little blue trunk that held and protected my few young-life's belongings.

Slowly and with ceremony—thinking about Homer's fingers touching those very same places—I pulled up the brass latches. I held my breath and raised the heavy lid knowing he had lifted that same lid many times before.

It was empty.

I was so very disappointed—I'd had such hopes.

Snap Beads

I left the trunk in the middle of my kitchen for a couple of days while I eyed its drab olive exterior, tarnished brass hardware, and worn, thick leather side-handles. It was made to withstand time and trouble. It was made to bear heavy burdens. Homer's name, rank, and serial number were stenciled on the side, and a partially peeled travel sticker dated April 3, 1955 remained below his name. Where had Homer been? Where was he going? I would have been a year old—I would have belonged to him then.

It called for my attention. I carefully washed and oiled the trunk inside and out until it gleamed. The brass and leather became beautiful. Inside there was a nested, lift-out drawer made of wood—richly grained and now-glowing—a purposeful place to hold and protect important things. I wondered: After years of knowing war and peace, of carrying and protecting fatigues and pressed uniforms, tins of black shoe polish, dog tags and medals, letters from home, and, perhaps, pictures of Melba and me—when had it emptied?

As I labored to make this unexpected gift beautiful again, bittersweet memories of Homer and Melba's young lives of temporary places, spans of separation, brief belongings, and difficult, complicated love filled me with wistful emotion.

That box wasn't empty after all. It contained memories—all that was left of three briefly connected lives.

47

Beginning From This Morning

ALICE SAID TIMIDLY TO the Gryphon and Mock Turtle: "I could tell you my Adventures—beginning from this morning... but it's no use going back to yesterday because I was a different person then."[4]

Like Lewis Carroll's figurative tale of Alice's journey, my narrative begins at the beginning—my metaphoric and literal morning. My autobiographical tale ends when I, too, am a different person, someone other than who I might have been. But unlike Alice's comment, "It's no use in going back to yesterday," by revisiting and relating the tale of my memories, by laying them side by side, I've found order, coherence, acceptance, and a greater sense of... self. Jerome Bruner writes: "The construction of selfhood... cannot proceed without a capacity to narrate. Once we are equipped with that capacity, we can produce a selfhood that joins us with others, that permits us to hark back selectively to our past while shaping ourselves for the possibilities of an imagined future."[5]

Here I am again, in real time, waiting by the curb. I'm trying to prepare my mind and emotions for an imagined future, a narrative of my aging self—my own denouement.

4. Carroll, *Alice's Adventures in Wonderland*, 76.
5. Bruner, *Making Stories*, 87.

Bibliography

Bruner, Jerome. *Making Stories.* New York: Farrar, Straus and Giroux, 2002.
Carroll, Lewis. *Alice's Adventures in Wonderland.* Reprint. Orinda: Seawolf, 2018.
Didion, Joan. *We Tell Ourselves Stories in Order to Live.* New York: Alfred A. Knopf, 2006.
Holland, Jeffery R. *Christ and the New Covenant.* Salt Lake City: Deseret Book, 2009.
Kukil, Karen, ed. *The Unabridged Journal of Sylvia Plath.* New York: Random House, 2000.
Welty, Eudora. *One Writer's Beginnings.* Cambridge: Harvard University Press, 1984.

www.ingramcontent.com/pod-product-compliance
Lightning Source LLC
Chambersburg PA
CBHW072200100426
42738CB00011BA/2486